THE VELVET UNDERGROUND

First published in 2022 by Palazzo Editions Ltd
15 Church Road
London, SW13 9HE
www.palazzoeditions.com

A CIP catalogue record for this book is available from
the British Library.

Hardback ISBN 978-1-78675-113-3

eBook ISBN 978-1-78675-077-8

Bound and printed in the UK

10 9 8 7 6 5 4 3 2 1

Designed by Sarah Pyke for Palazzo Editions

CHRIS ROBERTS

THE VELVET
UNDERGROUND

CONTENTS

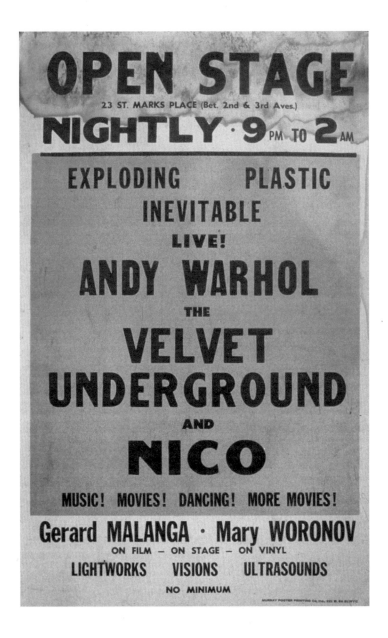

Here she comes now: the Exploding Plastic Inevitable, poster for St Mark's Place show

1
INTRODUCTION:
THE GIFT

As The Velvet Underground first toured America with Andy Warhol's *Exploding Plastic Inevitable* in 1966, the response was appropriately intense. "A three-ring psychosis that assaults the senses," declared *Variety*. "Screeching rock'n'roll which reminded viewers of nothing so much as Berlin in the decadent 30s," reckoned *Los Angeles Magazine*. "The most violent, loudest, and most dynamic platform for this new art," said *Village Voice*. The *Los Angeles Times* suggested that "not since the Titanic ran into that iceberg has there been such a collision. For once a Happening really happened."

The Velvet Underground happened, and their legacy continues to happen. They have always represented an incomparable mix of dirty realism and fabulous mythology. I interviewed the late Lou Reed three times and he was every bit as cantankerous and challenging as the mythology suggests. The first time we met, he drawled, "Oh, you started so well—but now these questions are getting really boring." The third time, I served up a softball opener, asking why he thought so many people were startled that he was collaborating with Metallica. "Who is??" he growled, eyeballing me sternly. "Who's startled? Who are these people? Name them! Who??"

On the middle occasion, in 2004, he was relatively sweet, although broaching the subject of his hallowed history woke the infamous grinch within. "Why would I go and listen to my old albums? That would be like jerking off. Do you read stuff you wrote years ago? No, right? Do something new. I'd rather listen to something new by somebody else that I've never heard before." He relented a little as we talked. "Follow the dotted line. Look, put all the songs together and it's certainly an autobiography. Just not necessarily mine."

He'd hinted at similar thoughts and themes in the past. "Passion—REALISM—was the key," Reed wrote some years after The Velvet Underground had wound up their initial explosion as the sixties expired. He wrote this in the liner notes to his solo album *Metal Machine Music*, itself no formulaic easy-listening fodder. "The records were letters. Real letters from me to certain other people. I'd harbored the hope that the intelligence that once inhabited novels and films would ingest rock. I was wrong." And yet the maxim persists (initiated by Brian Eno) that although not many people bought a record by The Velvet Underground, whose formative incarnation burned brightly but briefly, all those who did formed a band. The influence of this most New York of musical creations rippled far and wide, tall as a Manhattan skyscraper, deep as the murkiest of tunnels.

"If you play the albums chronologically," Reed went on, "they cover the growth of us as people from here to there, and in there is a tale for everybody in case they want to know what they can do to survive the scenes. If you line the songs up and play them, you should be able to relate, and not feel alone. I think it's important that people don't feel alone."

The Velvet Underground, for a time, made Reed feel less alone. And while his words and voice (predominantly) characterized the foreground of their sound (though Nico's tones provided a contrasting flavor at first), it was the chemistry sparked by the coming together and scratching against each other of its distinct individuals which gave them their unique edge and pioneering power. Technically, they only existed as a band for a few years (discounting reunions), but spoke volumes, contained multitudes. One of the most influential groups in rock history, they broke new territory, marrying pure urban rock 'n' roll energy with avant-garde sonic exploration; bringing sex, theater, and a kind of gritty cinema verité into their lyrics, and bewildering the mainstream just as they—as time went by—thrilled generations of outsiders.

Their prophetic debut album has been described as one of the most important musical works of the twentieth century, and it's not even everybody's idea of their best. And while the music has maintained its impact, against all odds, the fables and legends and anecdotes around the band and their circle have fueled equally resonant fountains of fascination. Reed and John Cale are among the most discussed and analyzed artists of their era, while an enigma persists around Sterling Morrison, Moe Tucker, and even Doug Yule. And if it's enigma you seek, Nico pretty much invented it. That's before you even get on to gazing at the interventions of Andy Warhol, Edie Sedgwick, The Factory and its Superstars, and the *Exploding Plastic Inevitable*. As David Bowie and many other key cultural figures whose muse was motivated by the Velvets and entourage may have mouthed while taking a tip or two: what a scene!

Their finding each other, or falling into each other, seemed both fortuitous and fated. Reed's life was already a tortured soap opera which could have been penned by Douglas Sirk and Hubert Selby Jr. when at nineteen the Brooklyn boy escaped to Syracuse University, studying literature and philosophy. His lecturer, the poet Delmore Schwartz, was an early hero, encouraging Reed's stabs at writing and warning him off "selling out." Reed got into jazz and drugs. He took a postgraduate course in drama, when, shortly after playing a dead body onstage, he met a guitarist, Sterling Morrison, and a friend called Jim Tucker whose sister Maureen liked to bash the drums. Student bands paid their dues in various permutations before Reed dodged the Vietnam draft—saying everyone he knew was doing so, and has since cited various reasons, from hepatitis to homosexuality to mental unfitness—and got a job with Pickwick Records in New York. Churning out jingles and ditties as a day job, he accidentally scored a minor hit under the name of The Primitives with "The Ostrich," intended as a parody of dance crazes. He cobbled together a band, including a friend's roommate, the classically trained son of a Welsh miner, John Cale; a former child prodigy on a scholarship to the prestigious music college Tanglewood.

"The Ostrich" didn't catch on, but Reed and Cale clicked. Along with Morrison they played as The Warlocks and then The Falling Spikes. Asked to contribute music to a short film based on *Venus In Furs*, Reed looked up the Sacher-Masoch book and threw himself into the idea. "Now," he groaned later, "everybody thinks I invented masochism." Upon discovering another "subversive" book, by Michael Leigh, the band knew they had their new name—The Velvet Underground. And following the departure of their original drummer, "Moe" Tucker was back in the story. "We needed an amplifier," deadpanned Reed. "And she had one." Greenwich Village clubs hosted them and then, in most cases, fired them. But not before Warhol had stumbled upon their show.

The radical Pop Art phenomenon offered them a management contract within days of meeting them in 1965. They weren't the types to be anybody's puppet, but Warhol was famous, hip, and would provide money, equipment, rehearsal space, and encouragement. They signed up. He planned events—happenings—at which they'd play. His cool, counterculture charisma was an astute match for theirs. They brought him darkness. He brought them light and heat.

"Andy told me that what we were doing with music was the same thing he was doing with painting, movies and writing," said Reed. "That is—not kidding around. We were doing a specific thing that was very, very real. It wasn't slick or a lie in any conceivable way. All the songs were written before I met him—it's just that they happened to match his thing perfectly." The band hung around Warhol's notorious silver-walled Factory with his flamboyant cohorts as additional inspiration. Andy insisted they were still missing something, and urged them to consider Nico, the German-born former model-actress (she appeared in Fellini's *La Dolce Vita*) as an onstage plus. Reed wasn't keen as she was a friend of Bob Dylan's, a perceived rival, but tolerated her to appease Andy. And when they started gigging together, especially at Warhol's "Up-Tight" mixed-media event, the city started buzzing. The *Exploding Plastic Inevitable* ensued, with strobes, spotlights, and writhing dancers accompanied by the Velvets' curious blend of dappled ballads and squalling feedback. "Revolutionary," claimed Warhol. "Fun," shrugged Reed.

Then came the recordings, with Warhol falsely credited as producer as a marketing technique. We'll delve into these in more depth in the book, but suffice to say there are few more canonical titles in art-rock history than the likes of "I'm Waiting for the Man,"

"All Tomorrow's Parties," "Heroin," "I'll Be Your Mirror," and "Sunday Morning," all of which graced the debut album, released just before The Beatles' *Sgt. Pepper*. And there are few more iconic album covers than Warhol's phallic banana. *The Velvet Underground and Nico* flopped, of course, as did second album *White Light/White Heat*, with its seventeen-minute one-take wonder "Sister Ray." Bickering and feuds broke out with Warhol and between the two justifiably large egos of Reed and Cale. "He's as stubborn and egocentric as I am," the perennially undervalued musical innovator Cale said. Something had to give. Turned out it was the Welshman, in 1968. Reed steered the group in a more melodic direction. Pronounced Cale later, "It was just a flash in the pan. It came and it went. We never really fulfilled our potential. But we defined a completely new way of working. It was without precedent. Drugs, and the fact that no-one gave a damn about us, meant we gave up on it too soon."

For the third album, *The Velvet Underground*, the young, malleable Doug Yule was brought in as Cale's replacement, although Reed largely told him what to do. Morrison began to chafe at the sentimentality creeping into Reed's love songs. Despite this, any record giving the world "Pale Blue Eyes," "What Goes On," and "Beginning to See the Light" can hardly be rated as less than extraordinary. And 1970's *Loaded* offered us "Sweet Jane," "Rock & Roll," and "Who Loves the Sun." Reed, however, was unhappy with it, and after a luckily recorded show at Max's Kansas City, he walked from this particular wild side, now paranoid, sleep-deprived, speed-addicted, and exhaustingly defensive. Doug Yule (often too harshly maligned) kept the name going with 1973's universally panned *Squeeze* album, but Reed was now planning a solo career with new allies like Bowie.

The seventies were moving on from the sixties. Cale too was carving out an important niche as a great musician and producer. The factual lifespan of the Velvets was over—until the brief, intriguing nineties reunions. And their cultural lifespan was just getting started . . .

"I'm stunned," Moe Tucker has offered, "by what people still think of us." "It was a process of elimination from the start," muttered Reed, looking back in tranquility. "First no more Andy, then no more Nico, then no more John, then no more Velvet Underground. If it wasn't me, I would have idolized myself in the Velvets. I loved what we did and I'm proud of it. We stood for everything that kids loved and parents hated. We were loud, we were vulgar; we sang about dope, sex, violence—you name it." He added disingenuously, "We didn't understand why everyone was reeling in shock."

Anti-hippies who shared more with the Beat Generation before them and the punks yet to come, the nocturnal, mostly black-clad and shades-wearing Velvets were, in Warhol terms, more electric chair than Marilyn pop. A cult outfit? Maybe now the biggest and best of all time. "It was uncharted waters," said Reed. "There was such a narrow-minded view of what a song could be." Their velvet was anything but smooth. Their underground changed the overground forever. Their legend and mythology will run, run, run. Until tomorrow, but that's just some other time.

As they proposed on the *VU* track "Temptation Inside Your Heart," "electricity comes from other planets."

When midnight comes around: Café Bizarre, West 3rd St, Greenwich Village, New York

2
TRAIN ROUND
THE BEND

Lou Reed

"I wouldn't call it the heart of darkness," mused Reed. "I'd call it the heart of illumination." He was talking to me about his divisive collaboration with Metallica, *Lulu*, in 2011. He could of course as easily have been describing his time with The Velvet Underground. In 1977, he told *Melody Maker*'s Allan Jones, "I've hidden behind the myth of Lou Reed for years. I can blame anything outrageous on him. I make believe sometimes that I'm Lou Reed. I'm so easily seduced by the public image of Lou Reed that I'm in love with Lou Reed myself. I think he's wonderful. No, it's not something I do to disguise my vulnerability or insecurity. Sometimes I just like being Lou Reed better than I like being anyone else."

The myth is important. It seems that Lewis Allan Reed was born in Brooklyn, New York, on March 2, 1942. But for a while back then, there were claims he was born Louis Firbank a year or two later in Freeport, Long Island. Such confusion and willful muddying of waters feeds the fantasy. In the seventies, when his record company were pressed by journalists for the true facts, they confessed they were afraid to pin him down on such matters. Moe Tucker's insistence that the first version held water held sway.

Reed had a younger sister, Merrill (born Margaret), and a brother ten years his junior. His father, Sidney Joseph Reed, born

1913, ran a legal accountancy firm; his mother, Toby (née Futterman), born 1920, is said to have been a former beauty queen. Sidney had changed his name from Rabinowitz to Reed. Lou drawled to *NY Rock* in 1998 that although he was born Jewish, his real god was rock 'n' roll.

Sidney's business went well. When Lou was eleven, the family moved upmarket from Brooklyn to Freeport, Long Island. Lou later claimed his parents were self-made millionaires, but added, "I didn't want to grow up like my old man." It's a stretch though, for all Lou's purported unhappiness, to see his childhood as a tough one. At least on the surface.

In Freeport he attended Atkinson Elementary School, then Freeport Junior High. His sister later told *Medium* that he suffered panic attacks, was generally awkward, and "possessed a fragile temperament." But having gamely tried sport and failed to transcend mediocrity—as the song goes, "I wanted to play football for the coach"—he got into music. His parents could afford his classical piano lessons. He studied theory, composition, the avant-garde. For the rest of his days he would either dismiss this technical grounding as "boring, I forgot it all," or flag it up proudly to display his credentials, depending on what kind of record he was releasing. He was also the kind of kid who writes poetry. With his cousin, he composed copies and pastiches of current doo-wop and rockabilly hits. He played in loose informal bands. Mastered the three chords that count. Got into drugs at sixteen.

His first recording was as a member of The Jades, a three-piece who'd previously been called The Shades. A performance at their school talent show was well received. They put out a double A-side

"So Blue" and "Leave Her for Me," both co-written by our young man Lewis Reed, and released by Time Records. It flopped, despite producer Bob Shad bringing in saxophonist King Curtis—soon to be known for such classics as Aretha Franklin's "Respect" and The Coasters' "Yakety Yak"—as a session player. It did get Reed his first ever radio play, but The Jades couldn't get past playing shopping malls. His parents were already questioning his choices.

They weren't thrilled that his sexual tastes weren't binary. He was having nervous breakdowns, his sister has said, displaying depression and anxiety as he tried to cover up his confusion. It was the late fifties; earlier in the decade, Senator McCarthy had instilled fear and loathing of "subversives" and "hoodlums." At sixteen or seventeen, had his family been more working-class, Reed might have taken a beating from his own father for homosexual tendencies. As they were well-off, they elected upon a course of action which at the time might have felt modern and progressive, to them, but which induces chills to read about now. After gleaning from a psychologist that they were inadequate parents, they took a risk. Three times a week, as recommended to them, they sent Lou for electroconvulsive therapy (ECT). "You lose your memory and become a vegetable," recalled Reed, angry at his father, and addressing the matter in the song "Kill Your Sons" (written long before its 1974 recorded version). At the very least, he was traumatized. Amateur psychologists can read volumes into the episode. From then on, Lou railed against parents, family, suburbia, society, and authority. He was ever prone to anger and mood swings, writing lyrics concerning pain, distress, and murky sexuality. And to latching on to a series of substitute father figures, at least for some years. (His sister has suggested that their parents were not homophobic, but that doctors had told them the ECT treatments would help Lou's mental health and "behavioral" issues.)

As the sixties began, he wanted to make something of himself. Notionally "recovered" from his treatment, he escaped to Syracuse University, two hundred miles north-west. Its alumni include President Joe Biden; writers like George Saunders, Joyce Carol Oates, Alice Sebold, and Aaron Sorkin; artist Bill Viola; actors Peter Falk and Vera Farmiga; and Eileen Collins, the first female commander of a space shuttle. Now aged nineteen, Reed studied a BA degree in journalism and creative writing, also taking an interest in philosophy and film. He also became a platoon leader in ROTC—the Reserve Officers' Training Corps—and later told *Time* magazine he wanted out so badly that he held a gun (unloaded) to his commanding officer's head. That worked. He was expelled from the corps. Debate goes on as to whether this was another case of Reed fanning his own mythology with some delicious apocrypha.

He devoured Hegel, Kierkegaard, and the French Existentialists. His favorite lecturer was Delmore Schwartz, a poet and author of some repute but in some decline. "The first great person I ever met," said Reed on an American Masters documentary. Schwartz had broken fresh ground with his 1937 short story "In Dreams Begin Responsibilities," but after early acclaim had become a somewhat frustrated, disgruntled, self-absorbed man. Reed's hero worship, it seems, rekindled some fire in him. He'd washed up at Syracuse for a lectureship post in 1962, thanks in part to the loyal support of Saul Bellow and Robert Lowell, but within forty-eight hours of arrival had been arrested for drunkenness. Reed loved to hear this sparkling raconteur regale the students in the bar with tales of the sex lives of James Joyce and T. S. Eliot. Schwartz responded, giving Reed signed copies of his books and encouraging him to get into Dostoevsky. He nurtured Reed's poetry, and hammered home that he should never "sell out." This early mentor was often cited as a primary influence by Reed, who namechecked him on future albums and dedicated the Velvets' "European Son" to him.

Lou's poetry met rejection slips from magazines, but he found another pleasurable release by hosting a late-night radio show on WAER, a Syracuse station situated on campus. He named his show "Excursions on a Wobbly Rail," after the song by free jazz pianist Cecil Taylor. This unlikely DJ (imagine that voice giving you time checks and weather updates) played plenty of free jazz, plus doo-wop, rhythm and blues, and Sun Records rock 'n' roll. Ornette Coleman and Don Cherry, both of whom he'd record with later, were favorites. His sister recalled (in *Medium*) after Lou's death: "He started a band; he had his own radio show. He reportedly libeled some student on his radio show: the kid's family tried to sue my father. And there were other extracurricular, possibly illegal activities of which the university didn't approve. I believe they tried to kick him out. But he was a genius: what could they do? He stayed and he graduated."

He hung out with fellow student Garland Jeffreys, a musician with whom he remained friends all his life. Jeffreys told *Syracuse. com*, "At four in the afternoon we'd all meet at the bar The Orange Grove. Me, Delmore and Lou. That would often be the center of the crew. And Delmore was the leader—our quiet leader." Lou also got into intravenous drugs, and developed hepatitis, allegedly from a shared needle. He'd later quip, "The Beatles were innocent of the world and its wicked ways, while I no longer possessed this pristine view. I, after all, had jaundice."

Despite all the complications he took a postgraduate course in first journalism then drama. Around this time he met Sterling Morrison and Moe Tucker, forming a student band that, according to Reed, made him more money than playing with the Velvets ever did. He officially graduated from Syracuse University's College of Arts and Sciences with a BA *cum laude* ("with distinction") in English in June 1964. He moved to New York City, where he landed a job at Pickwick Records as an in-house songwriter.

No sell-out? Here, while he continued working on his own stuff in his own time, his job was to rattle out jingles, ditties, parodies and rip-offs of current hits, to be flogged on supermarket-targeted albums under fictitious band names such as The Roughnecks, The Beachnuts, The All Night Workers. One of these, The Primitives, scored minor success, which led to a potentially awkward scenario as they were invited onto the popular TV show *American Bandstand* to perform their catchy number "The Ostrich." This was a faux-exuberant spoof of the burgeoning boom in dance crazes, with Reed's brand of sarcasm showing youthful form in lines suggesting you do the ostrich by following commands like "put your head on the floor and have somebody step on it." He and colleague Terry Phillips cobbled together an ad hoc lineup to play the song, with two guys Terry met at a party. Tony Conrad was one. His roommate, John Cale, the other.

The Primitives and their ostrich fixation didn't last too long, but Cale's interest in the avant-garde—he was playing viola in La Monte Young's Theatre of Eternal Music—captivated Reed. Equally, Cale had been intrigued to see that for "The Ostrich," Reed tuned all his guitar strings to the same note. This, the group came to call "the ostrich tuning." It created a drone effect not dissimilar to some of the experiments Cale and Conrad had been involved with in Young's experimental ensemble. The pair continued to collaborate, inviting Reed's college acquaintance Sterling Morrison and Cale's neighbor, poet and percussionist Angus MacLise, to join them. Through '65 they played under short-lived names like The Warlocks and The Falling Spikes.

A high school friend of MacLise, Piero Heliczer, who was by now an underground filmmaker, asked them to contribute music for a short film he'd made called *Venus in Furs*. Reed looked at the book of the same name by Leopold von Sacher-Masoch, and thought this a terrific idea. MacLise disappeared. Maureen "Moe" Tucker returned. This foursome—Reed, Morrison, Cale, and Tucker—played their first ever show at Summit High School, New Jersey, on December 12, 1965, supporting a band called Myddle Class (*sic*).

Another subversive book was shown to Reed and Cale by Tony Conrad. It was Michael Leigh's meretricious sex exposé, *The Velvet Underground*. All agreed this would make a fine name for their new band. They played a few nights at the Cafe Bizarre in Greenwich Village, their set a curious mixture of Chuck Berry chestnuts and Reed's darkly worded songs arranged with Cale's curious musical twists. They were soon sacked by the venue, but not before Andy Warhol had seen them there. From 1966, he helped them warp history.

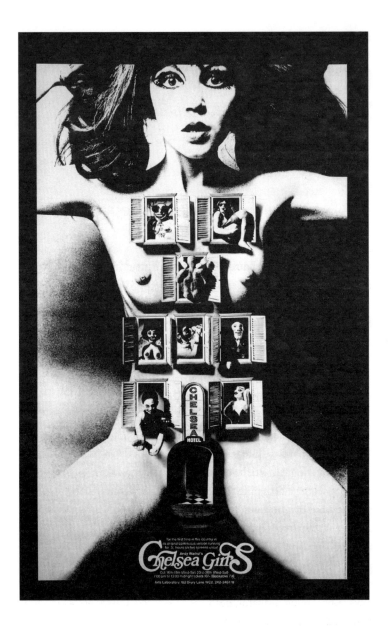

She wants another scene: poster for *Chelsea Girls*, the 1966 Andy Warhol/
Paul Morrissey film.

3
ONE OF
THESE DAYS

John, Nico, Sterling, Moe, Andy, and Other Superstars

John Cale OBE has had an even more interesting life than you imagine.
The son of coal miner Will Cale and school teacher Margaret Davies,
John Davies Cale was as valleys-born Welsh as they come, and yet a
complete one-off. To be born Welsh, goes the slogan adapted from a
1967 Brian Harris poem, is to be born privileged—not with a silver
spoon in your mouth, but with music in your heart and poetry in your
soul. These he had in abundance.

Cale was born precisely one week after Lou Reed, on March 9,
1942. His birthplace, was the tiny village of Garnant in the Amman
Valley in Carmarthenshire, twelve miles north of Swansea. Cale's father
spoke only English. His mother (like many a working-class Welsh
mother wishing a better life for her children by stressing the importance
of education) taught young John and spoke to him only in Welsh, which
didn't help the frosty father–son relationship, although the boy began
learning English at school at seven. It was at that age, too, that he started
playing piano. Something of a musical child prodigy, he was performing
on the radio before he hit his teens. His mother tried to usher him
toward becoming a doctor, desperate for him to work anywhere but
down the mines. He, however, had the music bug.

He played the piano at all hours, practiced on the church organ,
and at grammar school, upon finding that the viola was the only free

instrument, picked that up too, quickly mastering it. He was already displaying an instinct to go against the grain. "Classical frowned on improv, so I frowned on classical," he told *Wales Online* in 2016. "Mozart and all that lot, you had to reference them in the most perfect and reverential way. Whereas I was always interested in new ways of doing things."

Less positively, he has told *Wales Online* among others that he was molested twice when he was around twelve. Once by an Anglican priest and once by a music tutor. He also had health issues. Bronchial infections and problems meant he was, perhaps misguidedly, given sedatives, and he's spoken of experiences of nervous breakdowns both in his teens and later in life.

He's described growing up in Wales as a "pretty draconian" experience with regard to religion, and has said he missed out on his teenage years, leading a "sheltered life, practicing scales instead of playing football." It wasn't always the happiest of childhoods: Music gave him a way to escape his worries. "I'd forever listen to foreign radio broadcasts: my mind was constantly wandering—the grass was always greener some place else, you know? Life was very uncomfortable, because she (his mother) banned the use of English in the house. That left me unable, really, to talk to my father. And my grandmother really ruled the roost at home—she didn't want me around at all," he continued. "What's more, she really didn't like the fact that my mum married an uneducated miner who didn't speak Welsh. It made for a lot of tension. What's odd is one of the things I vividly remember was my mother sitting down to read the obituaries in the local paper, to see if anyone she knew had died. I used to think: Oh man, I gotta get out of here . . ."

He wasted little time moving toward this goal. At thirteen he played with the Welsh Youth Orchestra, touring Holland as well as his homeland. He fancied becoming an orchestral conductor. And he got into less classical, more "teenage" music, listening to rock 'n' roll on the radio (for a while he styled himself as a Teddy Boy) but also falling in love with experimentalists like John Coltrane or near-namesake John Cage. He dreamed of New York, or his fantasy of it, as the most exotic and seductive place in the world. "The notion of New York as this 24-hour society where you could work as long as you liked, stay up as long as you liked, was fascinating to me . . . So to end up in America had always been my aim, even before I got an offer to go there."

First, he moved to the not-yet-quite 24-hour society of early sixties London, to study music at Goldsmiths' College, on a teaching scholarship. He had no real desire to become a teacher, and again felt boxed in by the traditional classical approach to music he encountered there. He did, however, enjoy learning more about Stockhausen, and even began exchanging letters with both John Cage and Aaron Copland. And he did get to conduct, helming the debut UK performance of Cage's *Concert for Piano and Orchestra*, with pianist Michael Garrett (who went on to score two Ken Russell films) soloing. Cale also became involved with Fluxus, the radical artistic community. He organized a concert for them, in July 1964, calling it A Little Festival of New Music, and had scores published in the collective's "Preview Review." He was a long way from the valleys already—making contacts, and starting to be noticed in, international avant-garde circles.

And so America, his dream, opened its arms to him.

When he left Goldsmiths', he'd won a Leonard Bernstein scholarship to study for two months in Tanglewood, Massachusetts, at the Berkshire Music Center, with Iannis Xenakis as his tutor. With that course completed, he realized to his delight that—without trying too hard—he'd been given a Green Card by US immigration, which meant he could stay on, living and working in the States for as long as he liked. Of course, he hotfooted it to New York, renting a loft apartment with the money he now didn't need for his return flight, and finding a job in a bookshop bearing the name Orientalia.

He was happily mingling and working with his heroes, who recognized his talents and vision. In late 1963, he and Cage were among a troupe of pianists who took shifts within an eighteen-hour marathon recital, the first ever attempted, of Erik Satie's *Vexations*. Each pianist played the 180-note piece 840 times. Cale appeared on the CBS TV panel show *I've Got a Secret*, where guests were challenged to deduce his amazing "secret": that he'd played in an eighteen-hour concert. A subsequent guest on the show was the only person who'd stayed for the entire performance. Another person, who'd been in the audience for some but not all of the duration, was Andy Warhol (not that Cale knew this until later). Repetition and—some might say— monotony were of course a key feature of Warhol's own aesthetic ethos. When a photograph of Cale and Cage together appeared in *The New York Times*, the Welshman's name was on the way to being made. Cage arranged for him to meet La Monte Young, who heard him play viola and invited him to become a member of his left-field musical ensemble Theatre of Eternal Music.

Legends of unpopular music, they are mostly forgotten in mainstream circles now, but this Fluxus-aligned group, part of Cage's "noise music" movement, released a dye which was to significantly permeate the Velvet Underground's colorings. Young, for his part, was quite the character. A Californian jazz saxophonist who'd discovered what wasn't yet labeled "world music," had a tendency to smash up instruments onstage and had been romantically involved with Yoko Ono. He'd gathered the restless talents of his wife, Marian Zazeela, on vocals, Angus MacLise on percussion, and Tony Conrad on violin, and created pieces with titles such as "Second Dream of the High Tension Line Stepdown Transformer." They were very, very loud, would sometimes sustain one note for two hours, and, in layman's terms, pretty much invented the musical concept of the drone, a key element of the Velvets' palette. With Cale joining, they came up with improvisations such as "The Tortoise (His Dreams and Journeys)." Again, Warhol witnessed one show, at a private party at the Metropolitan Museum of Art. Jackie Kennedy was also among those struggling to whistle along.

Cale continued to work with Young even after he met Lou Reed and the Velvets gang, but bade his farewell after eighteen enlightening months in '65 as the Velvets emerged from their rehearsal cocoon. He and Conrad had also formed a sidebar duo called The Dream Syndicate (a name purloined in the eighties by a West Coast "Paisley underground" rock outfit). They did counterintuitive things, not just with their sounds but with their physical instruments, with Cale radicalizing his viola's shape and structure. They'd also compose scores for underground films by alternative director Jack Smith.

The connection with La Monte Young also brought Cale another kind of adventure. Young funded his enterprise, allegedly, by dealing marijuana, and when Cale (also "allegedly") helped out, he was arrested, spending one night in jail. Charges were dropped. He was also fortunate that, considering he had a Green Card, he wasn't drafted to go to fight in Vietnam. A physical exam in early 1964 resulted in his being dismissed on medical grounds. According to Tim Mitchell's biography, hepatitis was cited. It's also conceivable, with a less rock 'n' roll spin, that the health issues of his youth were never satisfactorily resolved.

"It's funny, but it was only after about a year of living there that someone explained to me why so many people in New York would just smile and nod at me," Cale reflected decades later, talking to *Wales Online* and still carrying a vivid Welsh accent. "It's because they couldn't understand a word I was saying . . ."

Much as this son of Wales found the avant-garde scene inspiring, he still hadn't lost his enthusiasm for the rapidly rising energies of rock 'n' roll. He enjoyed the "British Invasion"—The Who, The Kinks, and Small Faces appealed to him as much as the now unavoidable Beatles and Stones. Tony Conrad and he moved into an apartment on the Lower East Side on Ludlow Street (with Angus MacLise—another La Monte Young peer—as a neighbor), and bonded further over a shared love of Phil Spector's Wall of Sound records. It was almost time for them to do the ostrich. Tomorrow was ready to party.

Nico

So enduringly powerful is Nico's mythology that when I tell people I met her, they get excited. They're rather less excited after I describe the bathos of the circumstances. In Manchester in the mid-eighties, I was sitting backstage after a gig by Buzzcocks pop-punk-poet Pete Shelley, nattering away drunkenly to God knows who. A large, low, subterranean voice behind me rumbled, "You are sitting on my coat." It was a voice which filled any room. As I turned, the voice, emanating from a visibly displeased yet simultaneously expressionless woman in black, stated slowly but highly effectively, "Get. Off. My. Coat." Within a second I'd clocked it was Nico, stood up, stepped aside, and said, "Oh, sorry!" Now that I was out of the way, I was no longer of interest to her. With hindsight, the coat probably had something she needed in the pockets. Anyway, a thrilling anecdote from la dolce vita there.

Federico Fellini's 1960 classic, *La Dolce Vita*, follows a journalist's existential struggle as, over a week in Rome, he strives to choose between the temptations of flashy self-indulgent excess and a deeper, more meaningful and reflective way of life. Now commonly cited as one of world cinema's greatest achievements, it was upon release described by *The New York Times*' critic Bosley Crowther as a "brilliantly graphic estimation of a whole swath of society in sad decay and, eventually, a withering commentary on the tragedy of the over-civilized." The director had "an uncanny eye for finding the offbeat and grotesque incident."

Nico was already twenty-one and a successful model when she appeared in it. In the scene usually referred to as "the party of the nobles," she meets up with star Marcello Mastroianni and other nocturnal friends and acquaintances of his on the Via Veneto. From here they're driven to an aristocrat's castle outside Rome, where the film's umpteenth hedonistic, intoxicated party is in progress. Marcello ultimately runs off with another woman—well, two—but Nico's brief appearance, more than a cameo yet less than a role, leaves a mark, her indefinable charisma evident. Fellini, his eye for the aesthetic of off-key beauty fully functioning, had spotted her on set and, inevitably charmed, offered her a part. Her chilly presence, burning-bright bangs, and smoldering monotone distinguished her from bubblier blondes. She stands out and apart, in her scenes, playing herself, radiating cool without trying at all. It helps that she can speak four languages and rock a simple black pantsuit, a rhinestone brooch, killer cheekbones, and a brooding intensity. She was born in Cologne, but that intensity was always too uniquely hers to be glibly categorized as "Teutonic."

La Dolce Vita still revels in a resonant cultural legacy six decades on. Referenced on screen by everything from *The Sopranos* to *Lost In Translation*, and in song by everyone from Bob Dylan ("Motorpsycho Nightmare") to Blondie ("Pretty Baby"), it's one of those rare style icons which is as interesting beneath the surface as on it. Nico, in her own way, bore a comparable duality.

Christa Päffgen's life was the stuff of legend and mystery even before she crossed paths with the Velvets. She has, at various times, been attributed with heritage as diverse as Hungarian and Spanish, but was indeed German. Having been born on October 16, 1938, at two years old she was moved from Cologne to the Spreewald forest area outside Berlin, the ravages of World War II affecting her parents' choices of location. Her father, Wilhelm, enlisted as a soldier, and some accounts say he was shot in the head by a French sniper in 1942. Some say he was then killed by a German officer who lacked compassion for the wounded. And other tales reckon the brain damage brought on by his shooting left him incapacitated and rotting away in a psychiatric institution. Others say he died in a concentration camp. The tragic-glamorous mist of rumor and apocrypha around Nico and her heritage was only getting started.

She herself gilded the lily, claiming on different occasions that her father was a Turk, a Sufi, a close friend of Gandhi, a spy, and an archaeologist born into a dynasty of Colognian master brewers. Of course, in reality, she'd barely have remembered him, if at all.

Her mother, along with her grandfather, brought her up. After the war, fleeing the Russian occupation, they moved into Berlin, making a home in the ruined, bomb-blasted American sector. "A desert of bricks," she called it. One has to assume the landscape and imagery affected her young worldview. Money was scarce. Leaving school in her early teens, she worked for a seamstress and selling lingerie in a high-end department store. By the time she was fifteen, her mother had helped her find assignments as a model with a Berlin fashion house.

Among other stories Nico told, she was, she said, raped at age thirteen by an American soldier. She testified at his trial on multiple rape charges: He was found guilty and executed. There are no records to confirm this, but then many such records went missing during that period. (She referenced the incident on her album *The End*.) The modeling career ushered in, at least for a while, happier times. The tall teenager's bookings soon took her from Berlin to Rome, Paris, and Ibiza (an island she loved all her life, dying there in 1988).

When she was around eighteen or nineteen, she changed her name to Nico. The most plausible explanation of the many she gave is that it was in honor of close friend Nico Papatakis, a Parisian nightclub owner whose boyfriend Herbert Tobias photographed her at a KaDeWe fashion show. She worked and socialized with this Nico for years, cohabiting with him sometimes. Herbert's passionate love for that Nico impressed her. She dyed her brown hair blonde— after Ernest Hemingway advised her to, she said. Again, it's more fun to believe Nico's fanciful claims than douse them with a pinch of salt. Now living in Paris, she posed for *Vogue*, *Elle*, *Tempo*, *Camera*, and many other magazines. Coco Chanel offered her a contract, but, never one to opt for the sensible career move, she hightailed it to New York, blowing that potential deal. She also shot TV ads and took small roles in the films *La Tempesta* (1958) and *For the First Time* (1959; starring Mario Lanza and Zsa Zsa Gabor). *La Dolce Vita* came next, by which time she was a New York resident.

She lived now with Nico Papatakis, and took singing lessons. She also took acting classes with acclaimed "father of method acting" Lee Strasberg. She was, she said, in the same class as Marilyn Monroe, which was "very exciting." Anecdotes are a girl's best friend.

She appeared in the Jean Paul Belmondo film *A Man Named Rocca*, directed by Jean Becker, as Villanova (shot by ex-gangster Belmondo), then as the lead in 1963's less-unsubtle-than-its-title *Strip-Tease*, directed by Jacques Poitrenaud. She even sang the title song, written by Serge Gainsbourg (but it wasn't released until a Gainsbourg compilation of 2001). In '62 she was the cover model for jazz pianist Bill Evans's album *Moon Beams*.

Something else happened in '62. On August 11, she became a mother. Having previously enjoyed a sapphic romance with actress Jeanne Moreau, she declared that French movie idol Alain Delon was the father of her son, Christian Aaron Päffgen (generally known as "Ari"). Delon always denied paternity. Ari was, however, eventually adopted by Delon's mother, who'd handled the lion's share of raising him, and he took her surname, Boulogne. Nico was now, it appeared, more interested in becoming a singer. (She did nevertheless bring Ari with her for much of her Velvets period, and reconciled with him again later.)

She made appearances at the Blue Angel nightclub in New York, offering her distinctive take on such standards as "My Funny Valentine" (which she recorded in the eighties). Yet what really got the ball rolling was her knack for connecting with movers and shakers. She took off for London, where she dated Brian Jones of the Rolling Stones. Jimmy Page played on and produced her May '65 debut single for Andrew Loog Oldham's Immediate label, "I'm Not Sayin'," a song written by Gordon Lightfoot. This was chosen by Morrissey as one of his Desert Island Discs in 2009, but hardly registered a presence upon release despite its stylistic similarities to Marianne Faithfull tracks of the era. She persevered, and after meeting Bob Dylan in Paris, recorded a demo of his song "I'll Keep It with Mine" for her subsequent solo album. She was waiting for her musical career to truly take off. (She later remembered meeting Andy Warhol and Gerard Malanga in Paris in the spring of '65. Malanga had told her to visit the Factory when she was back in town. In November she and her three-year-old son returned to Manhattan.)

Confident as ever, she presented Warhol with a copy of her single, and it was now Factory man Paul Morrissey who came up with the idea of teaming her up with the Velvets. She was "the most beautiful creature who ever lived," he mused. Warhol instantly cast her in his own films, from 1966's *The Closet* through five more, including most notably *Chelsea Girls*. He called her "mysterious and European, a real moon goddess type." Paul Morrissey thought the Velvets needed a front person "with a bit of charisma." Lou Reed was initially, of course, underwhelmed and somewhat insulted. John Cale has said she was deaf in one ear, which wasn't ideal for her singing, and arguably a problem for a budding chanteuse. "She was this gorgeous apparition," recalled Maureen Tucker. "I mean, she was really beautiful." One critic, Richard Goldstein, posited that her stage presence was "half goddess, half icicle."

Another, *IN New York*'s Pat Patterson, asked her in 1966 for the liner notes to her album *Chelsea Girl* how long she'd been singing. "'Well, yes,' she said, but instead of continuing she stopped and seemed to search back past all the timeless cop-outs, past the obvious to what she really did think. 'I don't see that it makes a difference,' she replied finally. 'Because every day I feel that the day before doesn't count . . . If tomorrow I find somebody who is pretty much like me, and I put her here to sing, she can be Nico while I go to do something else.'"

Sterling Morrison and Moe Tucker

Thirty miles from Manhattan you'll find East Meadow, a hamlet in Nassau County (Long Island), New York State, where it's rumored George Washington spent one night in 1790. Getty Oil is based there; Snapple and Lufthansa US used to be. Eleanor Roosevelt spent some of her childhood living there, and it's given the world Mountain vocalist Leslie West and the actor William Fichtner. On August 29, 1942, it gave us Holmes Sterling Morrison Jr., the often under-celebrated guitarist with The Velvet Underground.

Sterling had two brothers and two sisters, but his parents divorced when he was young, his mother remarrying. Technically, his schooldays bore witness to the first ever meeting of two Velvet Underground members, as he and Maureen Tucker's brother, Jim, attended Division Avenue High in nearby Levittown, Sterling and Maureen thus crossing paths at a young age. Sterling had learned the trumpet at an even younger age, and before he hit his teens was a keen guitarist. After a stint at Syracuse, he went on to major in English at New York's City College, but had an encounter with Lou Reed while visiting Jim Tucker at the former university. They briefly bonded over blues and doo-wop, Morrison considering Reed to be a fellow one of "the lunatic fringe."

"When I was a student at Syracuse," he told TV show *The Velvet Underground: Feedback* in 1986, "I was just in my room late one night playing records with two friends. We had old blues records—Ray Charles, Lightnin' Hopkins ... And suddenly there came a knock on the door. We thought it was the person in charge of the dormitory, coming down to complain, because that's usually what happened. Instead, it was the guy upstairs, who turned out to be Lou. And he needed records, for his campus radio show. He was running out of blues, and that sort of thing, and my room-mate Bob Davison was a big collector. And I had my things too. So Lou borrowed some records. And that's where we first met. We made plans, but he was kicked off the radio show before we ever did much of that.

"Lou was pretty guarded about himself, but he did let it be known that he was an English major and that he liked to write poetry. But he didn't say anything about playing music. And then one day, the ROTC military training program that they have in colleges, where they have people out marching around in a big field behind the dorms, was on ... and suddenly we could hear this real loud humming and buzzing upstairs. It was somebody playing electric guitar at full volume. So then I knew that Lou was a guitar player too! And we just went from there ..."

Sterling had played in various bands—"some of the shittiest bands that ever were"—but wasn't overly invested. He and Lou moved on until they were fatefully brought together again in New York when Reed and Cale recruited him to their new baby.

Maureen Ann Tucker had been ten when she met Sterling. Born August 26, 1944, in Jackson Heights, Queens, she grew up in Levittown. Her family has been described as middle class and Catholic: Dad James was a house painter and mum Margaret a clerk. (Echoes of Reed's lyrics get everywhere, don't they?) Her big brother, Jim, introduced her to Sterling: They had a sister, Margo, too. Like the Velvets males she'd listen to Murray the K's radio show, loving the new exciting rock 'n' roll sounds and becoming a fan of Bo Diddley and the early Rolling Stones. Less typically, she also developed a taste for the music of Babatunde Olatunji, the Nigerian percussionist and activist. She dabbled in the clarinet and guitar, but in her late teens took to playing along to the radio on the drums, improvising without any formal training on a second-hand kit. That kit helped her land the gig of gigs, when a local band she played in, The Intruders, split, and the Velvets called. "At that point I was the only one they could grab, the only one with a drum kit." Sterling had remembered her. For their formative months, she didn't give up her own job as a data-entry clerk, commuting from Levittown to New York for their nocturnal events. Although with hindsight Lou Reed was to hail her as an all-time drumming genius, and her unconventional minimalist style proved influential, the band had misgivings about her talents early on. On the other hand, she had a car, which boosted her standing, and her almost androgynous tomboy appearance endeared her to the Andy Warhol crowd. Andy Who?

Andy Warhol

"I had three nervous breakdowns when I was a child, spaced a year apart," wrote Andy Warhol at the beginning of his 1975 book, *The Philosophy of Andy Warhol (From A to B & Back Again)*. "One when I was eight, one at nine, and one at ten. The attacks—St. Vitus Dance—always started on the first day of summer vacation. I don't know what this meant. I would spend all summer listening to the radio and lying in bed with my Charlie McCarthy doll and my un-cut-out cut-out paper dolls all over the spread and under the pillow."

He was to become a doll master, a puppeteer, but also arguably the most influential artist of the second half of the twentieth century, and although his involvement with The Velvet Underground was in some ways minimal, it was in crucial ways pivotal.

Andy was born in Pittsburgh, Pennsylvania, on August 6, 1928, to parents who had emigrated from what's now called Slovakia. (Mikó, now called Miková, was then in Austria-Hungary.) He was their fourth child, their first having died before they moved to the States. His father, Ondrej Warhola, arrived in 1914, Americanizing his name later to Andrew Warhola Sr. He worked in a coal mine. Andy's mother, Julia, joined him there in 1921 after her parents died. The family, living in the Oakland neighborhood of Pittsburgh, attended the Byzantine Catholic Church. Andy's two older brothers were Pavol (Paul) and Jan.

St. Vitus's Dance (formally known as Sydenham's chorea) first hit Andy in third grade. He had scarlet fever and rheumatic fever too. His skin went pale and his eyesight was poor, requiring dark glasses. Confined to bed, he lost himself in a fantasy world of drawing, of gazing at movie-star photos and of songs buzzing through the radio. A loner. An outcast from school bonding sessions. "I wasn't amazingly popular, but I had some nice friends . . . I wasn't very close to anyone . . . I felt left out . . ." The influence on his subsequent talents and persona is clear: He was socially unconventional—shy is too simple a term—but loved to arrange glamour, to dress the set of the life around him, to coordinate the movements of the more robust.

His father died in an accident when Andy was thirteen. He was "often away on business trips to the coal mines," according to Andy's writings, so he'd never seen him much. He recalls his mother reading *Dick Tracy* to him in a thick accent, and giving him a Hershey bar every time he finished a page in his coloring book. High-school days involved long walks. He had one summer job in a department store, which was spent "looking through *Vogue*s and *Harper's Bazaar*s and European fashion magazines."

At seventeen he graduated from Schenley High School, having won a Scholastic Art & Writing Award. Other notable alumni from the school include musician George Benson, Washington Redskins football star Larry Brown, and Jimi Hendrix/Little Richard bassist Billy Cox. (It was also the location for the 2015 film *Me and Earl and the Dying Girl.*) Andy planned to become an art teacher by taking a course in art education, but when he got to Pittsburgh's Carnegie Institute of Technology (now Carnegie Mellon University), he ultimately studied commercial art, graduating in 1949 with a BFA in pictorial design. In his time there he did make some efforts and inroads toward fitting in with others—on campus he joined the Beaux Arts Society and the Modern Dance Club. More significantly, as art director of *Cano*, the student art magazine, his illustrations and covers were his debut, his first published works.

Yet the fifties—and New York—brought him a new and invigorated life. Manhattan's Broadway boogie-woogie and the world of magazine advertising illustration offered him an instant sense of purpose, rhythm, and aesthetic belonging. If Pop Art, by Warhol's own estimation in his 1980 book, *Popism*, co-written with friend Pat Hackett, "first came out in New York" in 1960, New York was, prior to that, already a-go-go. "The art scene here had so much going for it that even all the stiff European types had to finally admit we were a part of world culture," he wrote. "Abstract Expressionism had already become an institution, and then, in the last part of the fifties, Jasper Johns and Bob Rauschenberg and others had begun to bring art back from abstraction and introspective stuff. Then Pop Art took the inside and put it outside, took the outside and put it inside."

With antennae as attuned as Reed's or Nico's to the art of self-mythology, Warhol wrote in *The Philosophy* that "when I was eighteen a friend stuffed me into a Kroger's shopping bag and took me to New York." He lived in a series of cockroach-infested shared apartments. "At one point I lived with seventeen different people in a basement apartment on 103rd Street and Manhattan Avenue, and not one person out of the seventeen ever shared a real problem with me." His "life in the 50s" was greetings cards and watercolors. He worked long hours. As soon as he stopped being desperate for success and became a loner addicted to television, he said, success happened.

He'd gained his first commission as the forties faded, drawing shoes for *Glamour* magazine. He now found work as a designer for shoe manufacturer Israel Miller. "Nobody drew shoes the way Andy did," said photographer John Coplans. He was already a character in the fashion world, known by some as "raggedy Andy" because of his studied, part-bohemian scruffy look. He was exhibiting in galleries as early as 1952, but things didn't really take off until he saw what Johns, Rauschenberg, and co. were doing and strived to put his own spin on it. He'd learned silk-screen printmaking techniques from Max Arthur Cohn, experimented with ink and tracing paper and an episcope, and early on learned that you could create limitless variations on a single theme.

He'd also developed a fruitful sideline as an album cover designer for RCA Records, often collaborating with another freelance, Sid Maurer, and working for graphic designer Reid Miles. Long before the Velvets' yellow banana, his work was adorning a wide range of record jackets, from jazz to classical. Trawling through these, you can witness his increasing adventurism, his desire to tweak convention and subvert the standard. The first—for Carlos Chavez's *A Program of Mexican Music*—appeared as early as 1949. His ink sketches decorated *Piano Music of Mendelssohn and Liszt* by Vladimir Horowitz two years later, and in 1953 he provided an apple with an arrow through it for a release of Rossini's *William Tell* Overture. His portrait of Count Basie for the bandleader's self-titled 1955 album is based on a photograph but clearly displays the artist's identity: Thelonious Monk and Kenny Burrell were among other jazz greats who could claim to have pre-empted the Velvets with their album cover art. Moondog's *The Story of Moondog* even used the calligraphy of Julia, Warhol's mother.

Julia had moved to New York in 1951 to look after Andy, living downstairs from him. He returned the favor by often using her handwriting as part of his art. She even won awards, including one from the American Institute of Graphic Arts for the Moondog cover. Julia illustrated books herself, frequently about cats, and was filmed by her son in '66 for *Mrs. Warhol*, a sixty-six-minute piece in which she played a blonde ageing movie star with many husbands. (As the seventies began, she moved back to Pittsburgh, dying in 1972.)

So Andy was perfectly placed to swagger, in his own peculiarly diffident manner, through the sixties. In July 1962, his first West Coast exhibition in L.A.'s Ferus Gallery introduced the Campbell's soup cans, and that November the Stable Gallery in New York was his first solo Pop Art show in town. The Marilyns, the Coke bottles, the dollar bills, the Brillo boxes and Elvises . . . all these icons, then iconoclastic, were up and running and making a big noise. His first film, *Sleep*, came in '63. He and other Pop artists were slammed for capitulating to consumerism. That evergreen rhetorical demand— What Is Art?—was being yelled anew.

In late '63, Andy moved into The Factory, on the fifth floor of 231 East 47th St in Midtown Manhattan. The rent? A hundred dollars per year. Over the next five years there, before the Factory moved, legends aplenty were made. He'd always worshipped celebrity, whether it was Monroe or Presley or even author Truman Capote, who he admitted to all but stalking. But now the nervous pale young man was a celebrity himself. His 1965 retrospective in Philadelphia saw shrieking fans mobbing him and his entourage. All the art from the museum's walls had to be removed for safety. So yes, there was no art to be seen. And yes, he now had an entourage. With them, he made more of his idiosyncratic, sometimes preternaturally dull, films—*Kiss*, *Blow Job*, *Empire* (a static view of the Empire State Building for eight hours). He was already keen to move between genres, between media. The *Exploding Plastic Inevitable*, a series of multimedia events—dance, light, noise—was the next logical, irrational, step. They needed a house band. "The counterculture, the subculture, pop, superstars, drugs, lights, discotheques—whatever we think of as 'young and with it'—probably started then," he wrote in *The Philosophy of Andy Warhol*, recalling this era. "There was always a party somewhere. In those days everything was extravagant . . . In the 60s everybody got interested in everybody else."

The Factory Superstars

"When we went up to The Factory it was a real eye-opener for me," John Cale told *The Guardian*'s art critic Jonathan Jones in 2002. "It wasn't called The Factory for nothing. It was where the assembly lines for the silk screens happened. And while one person was making a silk screen, somebody else would be filming a screen test. Every day something new. I think he was dipping into anything he fancied."

Less charitably, photographer Nat Finkelstein recalled that "Andy bestrode his world like a bleached blond colossus. I witnessed the birth of a monster: a silver sprayed black widow spider—fucking them over, sucking them dry and spitting them out."

Ultimately, the Factory fizzed and fermented in three different Manhattan locations, but the East 47th St loft hosted the pop history from '62 to '67. The silver pressure cooker turned silver after Warhol went to a party at photographer Billy Name's apartment, saw what Billy had done there with tinfoil and silver paint, and asked him to decorate his place the same way. This Billy did, using also some fractured mirrors. He even silvered the interior of the elevator.

Warhol did of course use the place as his studio, making prints and paintings and work in multiple genres to cash in on his booming brand name. More films followed. His silk-screen portraits rocketed in commission price, thus bankrolling the follies, high jinks, and flashes of genius which the Factory birthed and bore witness to.

What became this legendary location most was its role as a sleepless, speed-fueled focal point for the artistic, the indulgent, and the wannabes. Decadent parties gathered the Warhol "superstars": Documented in part in Reed's "A Walk on the Wild Side," these socialites, drug addicts, drag queens, divas, musicians, actors, and outside-of-society anti-establishment "free thinkers" helped Warhol create paintings and lithographs, make transgressive conservative-confounding films, and—most importantly—enabled the atmosphere in which this demimonde thrived. Sexual radicalism, "happenings," "free love." Billy Name, now resident, found a red couch on the pavement one night and brought that in: Guests from the famous to the fleeting would crash on it. It's seen in several of the studio's most celebrated films and photographs.

"He [Andy] was very easy to get close to," Cale told *The Guardian.* "Everybody had a real suspicion of Andy, but it was intellectual envy. We used intellectual envy as a self-protective mechanism more than anything else."

Among those who visited the Factory were Truman Capote (Warhol's crush), Bob Dylan, the Stones, Salvador Dali, Allen Ginsberg. Yet it was the Superstars who served as this benevolent nocturnal vampire's life blood: Candy Darling, Joe Dallesandro, Eric Emerson, Holly Woodlawn, Ultra Violet, Viva, Ondine, International Velvet, Ingrid Superstar, Taylor Mead, and other eccentrics and exhibitionists were as flamboyant as Warhol was withdrawn. Billy Name was a key figure, as were Gerard Malanga and Paul Morrissey, who did much of the heavy lifting while Andy generally took the credit. Probably the defining bright light who burned out was Edie Sedgwick, the "It Girl" and "Youthquaker" who embodied the Warhol Factory's glamour and danger, sex appeal and sadness. She would of course be a major muse and more for the Velvets.

Cale again: "The band had written the first album before we met Andy. He found us very much in the raw and gave us the protective shield we needed. We adamantly went our own way and made things very difficult for ourselves. We drifted off into this netherworld of art and music and film. Everybody on the Lower East Side was trying to do the same thing: destroy the formality of the audience. We found a location and an atmosphere that were very conducive. Andy was not a musician—it was more of an . . . intellectual camaraderie. We would travel around with his entourage. Edie Sedgwick would take us all out and pay the bill."

The Silver Dream Factory, as it was originally known before all involved abbreviated its name for convenience, was 50 feet by 100 feet, and had mutated from a simple hang-out for homosexuals and speed freaks (usually visiting Billy) to a modern-day Algonquin Round Table, albeit with sexual liberation and scandal more likely to happen than honed wit and badinage. Everybody wanted to be a Superstar, and every Superstar wanted to be in Warhol's movies. They were fame junkies, drawn like moths to a flame by the currency of celebrity, but there was among the scenesters a genuine affection for Andy. He was completely non-judgmental, more than content to be the city's most encouraged voyeur, with everyone competing for his attention. A workaholic himself, he preferred the hunger and greed for the spotlight of these untrained actors to anything resembling what most would view as talent. The relentless circus of sex, drugs, and casualties would have fascinated and transfixed him. Plus, no longer the lonely guy, he just loved having company.

"Do Not Enter Unless You Are Expected" read the sign on the door. It was one of the most pointless and ignored signs in the state. "Nobody normal would go near The Factory," said Cale. "It was a protective environment for kooks. Quite dangerous for your sanity."

Counterintuitively, the music, playing loud, was more often than not opera. Reed said, "It was like landing in heaven."

So how did The Velvet Underground come to land there and lift off?

Andy Warhol and Edie Sedgwick, "It Girl", "Youthquaker" and 1965's "Girl Of The Year".

4
FOGGY NOTION: BEGINNING TO SEE THE LIGHT...

Time for the ostrich to lift its head from the sand. Aside from their atypical *American Bandstand* experience, The Primitives—not to be confused with the Coventry indie band fronted by Tracy who crashed into the UK charts in the late eighties—may have peaked, with shows at a school and a supermarket, but the musical bond between Lou and John which later led to so much ambitious anti-pop was forged, primarily, through their easy competence in creating knowingly lightweight pop. Of course, they didn't want to do things the easy way.

"John was really impressed with Lou because Lou had this unique ability to sing lyrics," Tony Conrad, Cale's roommate and musical associate, told Spanish interviewer Ignacio Julia. "He would go out there without anything in his head at all and just sing songs. Lyrics would just come out of his mouth. You didn't know where they came from but suddenly he was doing rock 'n' roll." When Lou finally left his parents' house and moved in with John at 56 Ludlow Street, replacing Conrad there, they bonded further over Hank Williams and the kind of rock 'n' roll records which Lou knew backwards but which were refreshing to John, still breaking out from and rebelling against his classical upbringing. Both had hungry, often self-destructive, impulses.

When Reed bumped into Sterling Morrison for the first time in years on the street, he enticed him over to the Reed–Cale home, with music (and drugs) ensuing. They guessed, not least from The Primitives' experiences, that the obviously commercial direction might not play to their strengths. So they invented, indulged, and improvised, MacLise rehearsing with them. They made some noise. All involved later recalled this period as exciting and often jubilant as they made fresh discoveries with no self-imposed sonic barriers.

Filmmaker Piero Heliczer, whose silent arthouse works ran in The Cinematheque in Lafayette Street, invited them to play at his screenings. (They also took small acting parts on occasion.) They also improvised there to Kenneth Anger's *Scorpio Rising* and Barbara Rubin's *Christmas on Earth*, and took part in mixed-media "happenings," where, as poetry and slide shows dueled, they played proudly topless with painted chests. You see, Warhol didn't invent everything for them. They chose band names like The Falling Spikes and The Warlocks, and Reed's nickname for Cale was Black Jack. Cale's for Reed? Lulu. Which gives an additional subtext to the final album release of his life, discussed later . . .

The young experimentalists recorded a demo, which picked up glimmerings of interest in London—Cale was still flying back to the UK intermittently—but a greater momentum came with another name change. This one mattered. The Warlocks became The Velvet Underground. Tony Conrad had brought the 1963 book by Michael Leigh in, having found it on the street, and this "documentary on the sexual corruption of our age," which might have been forgotten by now were it not for this lucky association, fed into their fantasies. More because they loved the underground art and film culture than dug S&M, but still. Morrison opined that the book was about "wife-swapping in suburbia." "We didn't have a name for the band so we'd make up a new one once a week," Sterling told Julia. "That went back to Lou's practice at Syracuse: all the bands got such a bad reputation so quickly that people would say don't hire that band again. So we just changed the name . . . same people, same songs. We thought The Velvet Underground was a good name because it had underground in it . . . we considered ourselves part of the underground film community. We had no connections with rock and roll as far as we were concerned." He went on, "So we said: we're not in rock and roll any more, we're out of it, we're finished. The name didn't have anything to do with the leather and whips and all that stuff, but people thought it did. *Venus in Furs* was completed before we met Andy, so that reinforced the associations with the book, that in fact we were trying to make some statement about S&M. That was wholly accidental. The book itself is incredibly stupid."

New York music journalist Al Aronowitz—one of many to have championed Bob Dylan, The Beatles, and the Stones, came to check them out. A friend of Allen Ginsberg, he offered them a gig, making gestures along the lines of wanting to manage them. Thus, The Velvet Underground made their first appearance under that name at Summit High School in Summit, New Jersey, as support to a band called The Myddle Class (*sic*). They were paid $75: total, not each. However, this fee prompted their first split, before they'd even played, because MacLise thought that being paid for art was wrong. He'd been reading a lot of Oriental philosophy and reasoned, somewhat idealistically, that any creativity which went along with the principles of capitalism was pretty much evil. He took umbrage at the other members' acceptance of the deal. And that's how a desperate Cale, Reed, and Morrison contacted Sterling's old pal

Jim Tucker and tracked down his sister Moe, who not only had a drum kit but an amplifier to boot. Oh, and a car. She was in. On December 11, 1965, the Velvets debuted. Hold on to your hats, 1966, here they come now!

That night, they played just three tracks—"There She Goes Again," "Venus in Furs," and "Heroin"—but two females in the audience fainted.

Aronowitz was delighted. He got them a two-week residency at Greenwich Village's Cafe Bizarre on West 3rd St, where he perhaps imagined they'd iron out some of the more problematic kinks in their sound through practice and honing. It was an unfashionable joint, which insisted Tucker use a tambourine in place of a drum kit. The Velvets played six sets a night, for five dollars each, and padded out their sets with Chuck Berry and Jimmy Reed covers. Soon after Christmas, they deliberately got themselves fired to avoid having to face New Year's Eve there. This they achieved by belting out "Black Angel's Death Song," a number they'd specifically been asked not to play, at a deranged, aggressive volume. A couple of days earlier, they'd met Andy Warhol.

Gerard Malanga had dropped by Cafe Bizarre to see this band he'd heard about from Barbara Rubin. They sounded in theory, to him, like a rock band but not like a rock band. He wasn't disappointed. Once there, his feet got to dancing. Gerard really liked to dance. To his surprise, Reed and Cale egged him on, finding audience engagement a welcome novelty. Malanga brought Paul Morrissey by, with a view to filming the band. Morrissey was aware that Warhol was actively seeking a band to promote as he mulled over opening up a club, or was at least encouraging his entourage to actively seek one. The next night, Morrissey and Malanga brought him along to see the Velvets. By New Year's Eve, the group was hanging out with Edie Sedgwick at a James Brown show at the Harlem Apollo. Their story was about to get up and do its thing.

Some Kinda Love: The Factory Years

Invited to the Factory on West 47th Street, the band were wowed and intrigued by the studio cum speed-driven social hang-out. Warhol put his money where his enigmatic silences were, buying them some new amps and equipment and allowing them to rehearse and write in a corner amid the silver walls, as cameras whirred and Pop Art was processed. They'd entered his arena, but they were a perfect fit under his patronage. "The first thing I liked about Andy was that he was very real," said Lou. Andy and reality were not always so in sync.

Lou and Sterling had now moved to a freezing cold apartment at 450 Grand Street, to which the new gang of would-be friends, Warhol and Edie included, retired on New Year's Eve after the Godfather of Funk's show and a detour to supportive writer/music-biz-type Danny Fields's place. The atmosphere that night was nervy, tense, rather than convivial. And soon further friction was induced when Warhol and Paul Morrissey insisted they incorporate into the band a new singer they'd "discovered," a German blonde named Nico.

Warhol had, upon first seeing the Velvets play, liked that the crowd left "dazed and damaged." Morrissey was, however, often at the wheel while Warhol both took on too many projects and stared into space, and his own pressing idea was to up the ante on the fusion of films and music. Morrissey was less impressed with Reed and

Cale, feeling they lacked visual charisma. They in turn were offended by Morrissey, as he played them Nico's single. Reed was hostile to the idea—and to Nico—from the word go. However, the management and recording deal offered tipped the scales and brought him around. He was also keenly aware of the publicity their link-up with Warhol would provide. He wasn't devoid of pragmatism.

Nico said it was rather a matter of Reed lacking confidence as a singer and front man. For her, this could be a viable backing band, she reasoned. Yet Reed wanted the name to reflect the band's dominance, so The Velvet Underground and Nico it was, with this title suggesting she was a featured guest artist. Somehow, a compromise which all could tolerate and try to work with was agreed upon. Aronowitz was pushed aside (to his regret, they'd never signed anything with him) and Warhol and Morrissey were now the Velvets' official managers. They'd get a 25 percent cut. This looked even better for the Factory duo when they landed free equipment in an endorsement deal, so they didn't even have to buy the amps. Short on experience but long on confidence, they were winging it as managers. That publicity factor though? That they were good at.

Reed clocked Warhol's work ethic. Despite the front of frosty-cool dissociation, Warhol churned out art/product prolifically. He'd daily ask Reed how many songs he'd written since the day before. "I'd ask him why he was working so hard," recalled Lou, "and he'd say 'Somebody's got to bring home the bacon.'" After all, there were plenty of greedy mouths to feed in the Factory. Andy would regularly take everybody out for dinner at day's end, before most of the retinue embarked upon another druggy night out at art openings and nightclubs. Cale recognized that Warhol was a catalyst. "I doubt that Lou would have continued investigating song subjects like he did without having some kind of outside support for that approach other than myself." Sterling Morrison was more quizzical, wondering if another band might have worked equally as well as "something he could work into his grandiose schemes for the show." But he also allowed that Andy encouraged "the confidence to keep doing what we were doing."

There were others busy doing what they were doing in the Factory. Billy Name may not have known it at the time, but his photographs were to become vital documents of life in and around one of the most acclaimed artists in history. His unadorned images from 1964 onwards offer candid insights into Warhol's activity during his most significant period. Name's contribution to the mythology of the silver studio is perhaps only recently receiving the applause it merits; more so since his death aged seventy-six in 2016. His photographs of the art, the people, the Superstars, Lou, the Velvets, Edie Sedgwick, the silver balloons, and the famous screen tests are stark but seemingly eternal. And the look of it all wouldn't have happened without his untrained, improvising eye.

Glenn O'Brien wrote in his introduction to *Billy Name: The Silver Age*, "Billy, who had been Andy's sometime lover, became his principal architect and decorator, his secretary, his archivist, studio manager, security man, night watchman and bouncer, his casting director, his handyman, his photographer, his electrician, his magician. Billy was the one Andy counted on." After visiting Billy's Lower East Side apartment, Warhol delegated him to arrange the styling of the fourth-floor loft. Billy had thus spent most of '64 doing the graft, adorning every inch of the place in silver foil or silver spray paint, "silverizing" the previously nondescript space, and thus giving a key chapter in the story of the avant-garde its visual keynote.

Given a Pentax Honeywell 35mm camera by Warhol, he swiftly made an art of a hobby. If '65 was the year Edie Sedgwick's aura dominated the scene, Billy captured it. If '66 saw the Velvets' charisma lead the way, Billy captured them. The dark glamour of his work is a close sibling to that of the Velvets' music.

His name wasn't Name, until it was. Born in Poughkeepsie in 1940, his real name was Billy Linich. Before associating with Andy he'd worked in theatrical lighting design, and shone his beams on dancers like Merce Cunningham and Lucinda Childs. He'd also contributed to Theatre of Eternal Music under the direction of the previously discussed La Monte Young, just before John Cale joined. There had also been shifts as a waiter, in which capacity Warhol first met him. The son of a barber, he supplemented his income by giving a decent haircut, too. Said Warhol in his diaries: "Billy had a manner that inspired confidence. He gave the impression of being generally creative, he dabbled in lights and papers and artists' materials . . . I picked up a lot from Billy."

As the in-house Factory photographer—Andy was more interested in making films—Billy needed somewhere to live. So he moved into a closet (some say toilet: print the legend) at the back of the studio, and converted one of the bathrooms into a darkroom, teaching himself how to process his shots.

"Silver makes everything disappear," said Warhol. Billy Name made the Factory and its inhabitants appear to frolic on the thin line between glamour and squalor. He also assisted Gerard Malanga on Warhol's silk screens, designed or had his photographs used on some of the Velvets' record sleeves, and, many have stated, had an affair with Lou Reed too. When the Factory switched locations in '68, he became a reclusive hermit in one room in the new place, with few noticing when he left and disappeared in 1970. There may be some poetic spin on this tale, but according to Warhol in *Popism* he did leave a note saying, "Andy—I am not here anymore but I am fine. Love, Billy." Warhol never saw him again. The darkroom was cleared out, painted white, and became the Xerox room. Billy returned to Poughkeepsie, where, having given up his rampant amphetamine intake, he lived for the rest of his life, his photos of the heady sixties gradually becoming more and more precious.

Gerard Malanga was equally important to the temperature and timbre of the scene. As a poet and photographer (and much besides) himself, he's both gained and lost from his immersion into the Factory. As Warhol's "assistant" in the silk-screening department, it's likely he not only handled most of the work but initiated ideas too. And then there was the dancing . . .

Born in the Bronx in 1943, he was a student and promising poet at Wagner College in Staten Island when he first met Andy. He dropped out to take up "a summer job that lasted seven years" beside Andy from '63 to '70. *The New York Times* in '92 called him Warhol's "most important associate." "I liked Gerard," wrote Andy in *Popism*. "He looked like a sweet kid, in sort of a permanent reverie, it seemed . . . he wrote a lot of poetry." He acted in Warhol films like *Kiss, Couch, Vinyl,* and *Chelsea Girls,* worked on the iconic Screen Tests, and his collaborations with the Velvets famously included his choreography for the *Exploding Plastic Inevitable,* about which more soon. He co-founded *Interview* magazine, with Warhol and

John Wilcock, in '69. His filmmaking, photography, and poetry have flourished ever since, and he co-authored *Up-tight*, the first book on the Velvets, with Victor Bockris in 1983. In the Factory era he carried a bullwhip with him at all hours, and his "whipdance" routine on the Velvets' stage—in his youth he'd danced, more innocently, on Alan Freed's *The Big Beat* TV show—survives as a leading signifier of their decadent mores.

Also reflected in the Factory's silver was Mary Woronov, Malanga's co-dancer in that *Venus in Furs* sequence. Or Mary Might, as she was then known. She too appeared in Warhol films before, unusually for a Superstar, going on to a successful, relatively more mainstream acting career. She can be seen in well-known Hollywood movies such as Roger Corman's *Death Race 2000*, *The Lady in Red*, *Rock 'n' Roll High School*, and *Dick Tracy*. (Her appearance in 1998 drama *Sweet Jane*, about a teenage heroin addict, may have been rather *too* knowing.) "Of all the girls at Warhol's Factory, I was the butch one," she told *L.A. Stories*. "I spent my nights at Max's Kansas City. I was the strong one."

Brigid Berlin might also have considered herself "butch." With family connections to the affluent Hearst empire, she'd mingled with her parents' celebrity friends since childhood. Meeting Warhol in '64, she moved to the Chelsea Hotel and threw herself into a new lifestyle. Adopting the name Brigid Polk, she led the amphetamine craze, acted—she notoriously injects herself in *Chelsea Girls*—and taped and recorded as much of the goings-on as she possibly could. Her tapes formed the basis of the subsequent Velvets album *Live at Max's Kansas City*. Her own art has grown in reputation in recent times.

Then there was Ondine—real name Bob Olivo—who was at the hub of the Factory's gay crowd, though not averse to the overlapping speed-freak scene. According to Warhol, he made it very hard for Reed to give up amphetamines. His often over-the-top acting steals numerous Warhol film scenes. And when we talk of Warhol films, it's only fair to note that Paul Morrissey technically made many of Warhol's later films, on top of managing Andy's business affairs. Without Morrissey's drive and discipline, it's plausible that we wouldn't know or revere half as much of Warhol's work today. Films like *Flesh*, *Trash*, and *Heat*, perceived as essential later chapters in the Warhol mythology, are Morrissey films.

Yet if Morrissey was the unsung get-things-done motivator in the camp, and the Velvets were to become the sound of it, it's indisputable that the face of the Factory scene was Edie Sedgwick. She was, declared Norman Mailer, "the spirit of the Sixties."

Hailed as the era's "It Girl" and by *Vogue* as the "Youthquaker," Edie blazed like a comet through her short, troubled life. Coming from a rich Californian family, she was in a psychiatric hospital (at her father's insistence) aged nineteen by '62. Two of her brothers died over the next three years. Almost as soon as she came into a large trust fund on her twenty-first birthday, the debutante moved to New York to pursue a career in modeling. At a party in '65 she met Warhol, and she began frequenting the Factory. "She'd been in a car accident and her right arm was in a cast," recalled Andy. Such a trifle wasn't going to stop her. She made cameos in a couple of his films and he soon saw her as a lead, a Superstar among Superstars. The title of *Poor Little Rich Girl* relays, perhaps, his perception of her.

Yet the media picked up on her as the glamorous and glitzy face of the scene. Her unique, counterintuitive style and redefinition of beauty—the black leotards and minidresses, the oversized earrings and emphasized, almost panda-like eye makeup, the way she cut her hair short and sprayed it silver—made her the perfect visual foil to Warhol himself. The two appeared everywhere together, pre-empting accelerated celebrity culture, at galleries, parties, openings, concerts.

"This was the year when the idea of 'modeling' held more excitement for a girl Edie's age than it ever had before," wrote Warhol in *Popism*. "It had always been glamorous to model, but now it could be outrageous too. Very soon, Edie would be innovating her own look that *Vogue*, *Time*, *Life* and the other magazines would photograph—those long, long earrings with dime-store T-shirts over dancer's tights, with a white mink coat thrown over it all." And they say the Velvets were influential on the look of "indie" . . .

Yet after the moment cooled and the Andy–Edie platonic romance deteriorated, so did Edie's health. She saw Bob Dylan as her savior and exit strategy, but his enthusiasm was more limited. She had a relationship with Bob Neuwirth, but her decline into drug dependency and depression continued. In and out of hospitals, by November 1971 she was dead, barbiturate intoxication the cause, at just twenty-eight. She had burned brightly, but for all the heady and hedonistic highlights, her story always seemed like a tragedy waiting to happen. "She had more problems than anybody I'd ever met," muttered Warhol in hindsight.

The photographs and films will recall the radiant, enigmatic star of mid-sixties young Manhattan; the songs she inspired include the Velvets' "Femme Fatale" and, it's been suggested, Dylan's "Just

Like a Woman." But the drugs were destroying her even then. She later didn't shy from blaming Warhol for egging her on, or passively observing as she fell. "Warhol really fucked up a great many people's lives," she said. "My introduction to heavy drugs came through the Factory." When she ran—into Dylan's rescuing arms—Warhol sneered to the playwright Robert Heide, "When do you think Edie will commit suicide? I hope she lets us know so we can film it." The John Palmer/David Weisman film *Ciao! Manhattan*, wherein Edie played a version of herself, Susan Superstar, almost did that. Its poster—"Speed! Madness! Flying Saucers!"—remains an icon of cool, swooned over more than the sketchy film, just as Edie in her golden phase is remembered as if immortal; her messy, crumbling years conveniently forgotten. In this or any recounting of the Velvet Underground story, she plays the part of a flame, giving off light, heat, and energy. "I'd seen Edie lighting candles once," wrote Warhol, "and from the absent-minded way she went about it, it was clearly a dangerous routine. I told her she shouldn't, but she naturally didn't listen. She always did exactly what she wanted."

Among these eccentric dramatis personae, the nascent Velvets fell into step, as much as one could, with Warhol and the Factory.

As the band tried to bed in Nico, it became clear this was not a natural match. She was keen to be the sole lead singer. Reed of course wasn't having that, but at Andy's pleading and behest he did start writing some softer, less frenetic ballads to suit her incomparable vocal stylings. "I'll Be Your Mirror," "Femme Fatale," and "All Tomorrow's Parties," were penned for her to deliver. (Cale's drones and burrs served as a counterpoint.) She sang, as Warhol famously put it, "like an IBM computer with a German accent."

Moe Tucker noted she was "this gorgeous apparition." Cale has said she was deaf in one ear, which led to pitching issues. Nico said that Reed never liked her anyway.

This all gets odder, as she and Reed then began an affair, even moving in together. It lasted two months. She described him during that period as "soft and lovely, not aggressive at all," even adding, at risk of calling into question the public image he'd establish, "You could just cuddle him." Sterling Morrison gave a more objective, distanced report. "You could say Lou was in love with her, but Lou Reed in love is kind of an abstract concept." It was Nico who brought the romance to an end. It's said she snarled unpleasantly after one argument, "I cannot make love to Jews any more." Nonetheless, Reed was now a convert to her peculiar talent, and what Cale called Lou's "psychological love songs" for her, which stand now as enduringly affecting classics, had revealed an extra dimension to his writing.

Meanwhile, Cale was having his own earthquake of a romance, spending six weeks cohabiting with Edie Sedgwick, who'd made a beeline for him almost as soon as he walked through the Factory's doors. Tensions, resentments, and jealousies were all around. It might be glib to say they informed the music, yet it's clear they did.

Onstage, Nico was not one for motion, a statuesque riddle inside an enigma playing dodgy tambourine, but she knew how to model a stance when not singing. She wore white, a deliberate, jarring contrast to the band's black clothes. Photographers and media loved her, which was good enough for Andy, but the fault lines on which this transient musical marriage were built were soon impossible to ignore. Against any kind of logic, it yet created a mesmerizing, delicious magic. As Iggy Pop said to German TV many years later, crystallizing their aura: "They were dark."

Their first recorded work of any kind as a quintet was a film shot of a rehearsal at the Factory. The project was interrupted by a visit from New York's finest, the police being not infrequent callers given the noise and general brouhaha occurring there night and day. It was modestly called *The Velvet Underground and Nico: A Symphony of Sound*.

They then revealed this symphony at their debut gig, the choice of venue being wonderfully orchestrated. The New York Society For Clinical Psychiatry was having its annual banquet at Delmonico's Hotel. It was about to find its sanity challenged. "The Chic Mystique of Andy Warhol" was promised them. In January '66, *The New York Times*'s Grace Glueck reported on the event. The Society, she wrote, "survived an invasion last night by Andy Warhol, Edie Sedgwick and a new rock 'n' roll group called 'The Velvet Underground.'" Her gloriously dry and funny piece catches the mayhem of the evening's ill-fitting entertainment. "Until the very last minute, neither group quite believed the other would show up."

"The 'factory,'" she wrote, "as any Warhol buff knows, is the big, silver-lined loft where he and his coterie make their underground films and help mass-produce Andy's art. What 'The Chic Mystique' was, nobody really explained." Films were shown as background to polite chat, but then music broke out, Andy and cameramen moving among the seated psychiatrists' tables as the Velvets roared. Halfway through dinner—"roast beef with string beans and small potatoes," noted Glueck—a "short-lived torture of cacophony," in the words of Dr. Campbell, the doctors' chairman, was heard. Many left early.

"Ridiculous, outrageous, painful," said a Dr. Weinstock. "Everything that's new doesn't necessarily have meaning. It seemed like a whole prison ward had escaped." (Later that year, the ensemble played at the wedding of clothes salesman Gary Norris and Randy Rossi, the bride given away by Warhol. "Hey, we're really witnessing something—it's history! History!" yelled a young female guest, according to reporter Linda Lamarre. "It's not the kind of wedding we had planned for our daughter," Mrs. Rossi said, as eerie screeches emitted from the stage." The groom's father sagely offered: "He's old enough to know his own mind.")

Spring continued with the next gig, at Cinematheque on 41st Street. This formed a part of Warhol's Up-Tight show (its name dreamed up by Barbara Rubin), wherein Malanga and Sedgwick danced and writhed, films by Warhol and Morrissey screened, Danny Williams choreographed migraine-inducing lights, and the Velvets screeched in their harshest mode. Representatives of the art world outnumbered laymen in the audience. The Velvets played "Run, Run, Run," "Heroin," and "Venus in Furs" within their set, and Nico, at her willful insistence, sang Bob Dylan's "I'll Keep It with Mine." Naturally, the band didn't like her singing another writer's song, and they soon began deliberately performing it badly until she gave up the idea. During "Venus in Furs," Gerard Malanga initiated his notorious "whip dance." Despite the crowd being more baffled than enthused, the Up-Tight show moved on, with Nico driving as unconventionally as she sang, to New Jersey then Ann Arbor.

Morrissey and Warhol now sought a venue they could call their own, where they could put on their concepts without jumping through other promoters' hoops. They curated Up-Tight at Paraphernalia, the hip boutique where Betsey Johnson's designs were prominent: John Cale liked her so much he later married her. Brian Jones was in attendance. And then, in April, Morrissey found The Dom. This venue was the former Polish National Social Hall on St. Mark's Place. Its formal name, Polsky Dom Narodny, was soon abbreviated for convenience by the Factory crew: "Dom" is, loosely, Polish for "Home." This area of the East Village, with a large Eastern European population, hadn't previously been a hip neighborhood. That, like much else touched by the hand of the Warhol–Velvets coalition, was to change.

The lease was signed the same day the first show there took place. In the afternoon, The Velvet Underground loaded their gear in. In the evening, the *Exploding Plastic Inevitable* began, realigning the boundaries of rock music forever. The advert in the *Village Voice* asked: "Do you want to dance and blow your mind with The Exploding Plastic Inevitable?"

"Fragments," said Melvyn Bragg on *The South Bank Show*'s 1986 Velvet Underground documentary, "became movements." Scenester Danny Fields told Ignacio Julia, "I preferred many times to close my eyes, rather than see this psychedelic light show travesty flashing on the group. To me it was the music. The great credit due to Andy is that he recognized it. He thought that they were great. They were great before Andy; they were great during Andy. And afterwards too. Andy might have created the Exploding Plastic Inevitable, but he didn't create the sound of the band. That was there long before. Lou's song concepts and lyrics were avant-garde . . . John really put the psychedelic air on it. I thought they were ahead of everybody. It's the only thing that ever swept me off my feet as music, since early Mahler. They were a revolution."

The *Exploding Plastic Inevitable* was, however, infinitely more than just a light show. It upped Up-Tight's ante: more aggressive, more untethered, more flamboyant. Gerard and Edie twisting and writhing and thrusting. A sensory overload, or overdose: induced hysteria the goal. Referred to by insiders as EPI, it was both bold and indulgent.

Morrissey would project the Warhol films. Gerard would reinvent interpretive dance with some permutation of not-exactly-shy characters like Edie, Ingrid Superstar, Ronnie Cutrone, or Mary Woronov. As the Velvets played "Venus in Furs," Malanga and Woronov would enact their S&M frolic, the former fawning at the feet of the latter, her boots, her leather whip. And as "Heroin" played, he'd mock-inject himself from an oversized plastic cake-icing syringe. Those lights? Slides, strobes, spotlights, all crisscrossing and breaking the "sensible" rules of lighting etiquette. From the Factory, someone brought along the big silver mirror ball—it spun above the band's heads, catching the lights and refracting them in a crazed, arbitrary, yet highly effective manner. Many believe that this was where the notion of the disco mirror ball was invented. Certainly, within weeks, every discotheque worth the name in New York had acquired one.

Reed said the reason the band began wearing shades was to protect themselves from all the lights and films, particularly the dizzying strobes. The man who ran the EPI light show, Danny Williams, would stare at strobes for hours, to see how much the human body could take. He later committed suicide. Everybody working for EPI at the Dom got paid one hundred dollars a night, from Lou, John,

Nico, and the band to the dancers. Legend has it they saved up all these wages in brown paper bags to pay for the first recording session. It's more likely things weren't that cut and dried, as on their opening night some opportunist had stolen all Lou's doo-wop singles from his minimum-security abode, while on another night Moe Tucker's drums were stolen. So she played rhythm on two adapted garbage cans for a few nights.

Sterling Morrison declared that "everything raged about us, without any control on our part." Nobody had ever seen anything like it (though of course nowadays, in the desensitized twenty-first century, in old footage it looks relatively tame). "It is Here and Now and The Future," wrote Jonas Mekas in *The Village Voice*. Most reviews of the shows were actually fairly (or unfairly) damning (see the inner sleeve of the debut album for evidence), but hype was moving like a forest fire. Warhol had been making noises about quitting fine art. Nico had her own glamorous fan club. Even Jackie Kennedy trekked down to the Dom to see her perform. Salvador Dali too; some claim he joined the Velvets onstage. Allen Ginsberg did, and chanted Hare Krishna mantras. The counterculture fell in love with the Village. "We all knew something revolutionary was happening, we just felt it," mused Warhol in *Popism*. "Things couldn't look this strange and new without some barrier being broken."

When the circus of catalysts traveled West the following month, however, its cool factor failed to translate. A trip to Los Angeles for a month, a rational enough idea on paper, turned out to be a multitiered disaster.

Arranged by Charlie Rothchild, the jaunt in early May saw an entourage of fourteen flown to L.A. and lodged at the Castle on the Hollywood Hills. The Castle was a mansion regularly hired by visiting rock bands, for around $500 a week. Gigs were booked from the 3rd through to the 28th.

The first show was at The Trip on Sunset Strip. Frank Zappa's Mothers of Invention were booked as support. Lou, unfortunately, loathed them. Nonetheless, the buzz and hype was functioning and a starry California crowd turned out, from psychedelic music's big names like members of The Byrds and John Phillips and Mama Cass, as well as The Doors' Jim Morrison, to actors like Ryan O'Neal. Gerard Malanga later claimed Morrison (who was to have an affair with Nico) stole his leather-trousered look. The celebrities left without raving about what they'd witnessed, and the second night saw a much smaller, less glitzy crowd. So the disgruntled band left the stage with their amps howling with feedback, and Gerard got arrested for possessing a whip in the street. On the third night, the police shut the club down, with accusations of disturbing the peace and "pornographic" activity.

The Velvets thought it best to remain at the Castle and hope the club was reopened. The Musicians' Union advised them to stay the whole month, as this would improve their legal rights toward getting paid. (As it transpired, they didn't get the money until three years later.) At least they spent some of the time fruitfully, recording tracks at TTG Studios which would form part of the debut album. At the tail end of May, with the Trip still closed, the EPI played two nights at The Fillmore in San Francisco. Peace and love still did not materialize. The New Yorkers clashed with Fillmore manager Bill Graham, and it was clear from the audience's frosty response that the Haight-Ashbury scene had very different ideals to the East Village set. Reed had drug issues leading to hepatitis, while Malanga's whip got him into trouble again, and the hippy capital of 1966 despised what they perceived as nihilistic negativity, come to poison their good vibrations. It was a hook-up made in hell: amphetamine versus marijuana; sidewalks versus sunshine. One review called the Velvets "musical masturbation."

Come June, Lou was hospitalized back in New York (his hepatitis was at first erroneously diagnosed as lupus). Nico left for a break in Ibiza, wondering what she'd got involved with. Andy and Morrissey set much of their focus to filming *Chelsea Girls*. There had been a gig in Chicago, with the eccentric (even by this social scene's standards) Angus MacLise returning to temporarily replace Lou and Maureen moving to bass, with John singing. While the media bemoaned the absence of the two lead singers, the audience, oddly, loved it, and they were given further bookings.

Back in Manhattan, the chaos kept costing as Warhol and Morrissey learned that they'd blown the chance to extend the lease on The Dom, and Albert Grossman, Bob Dylan's manager, had smartly snapped it up while they'd been looking the other way. The venue was renamed Balloon Farm, and then the Electric Circus, and enjoyed great success in the heart of the new cool neighborhood. This missed opportunity by the Warhol camp had serious financial repercussions, which were to affect the Velvets' first record. Believe it or not, amid the mayhem, they had now recorded an album. A groundbreaking mix of beauty and a burrowing deep, deep underground, it wasn't devoid of mayhem itself. Or as British publication *Disc and Music Echo*'s uncredited reviewer put it on November 18, 1967, "For a long time we've been hearing a lot of groovy music all about peace and love from West Coast groups. This Underground is an East Coast, New York, group whose material is largely taken from the opposite side of life—evil and ugliness." The writer warmed to their theme. "Their music is hard rock 'n' roll brought up to date with electricity. An electric viola adds a distinctive, cruel, harsh note—it's particularly evil on 'Venus in Furs,' and 'Heroin,' two of the best tracks on the album, which are never likely to get played by the BBC. The drummer is a girl, the lead singer often sounds like Dylan and the beautiful Nico sings sweetly on the strange 'Femme Fatale,' and the lovely 'I'll Be Your Mirror.'"

Released in March of that year, the album was largely ignored, at least at first, by critics. Small US publication *Vibrations*, on its second issue, called it "a fully-fledged attack on the ears and on the brain." The record's inner sleeve proudly or perversely carried live reviews of the *Exploding Plastic Inevitable* which ranged from "the flowers of evil are in full bloom" (*Chicago Daily News*) to "the whole sound seems to be a product of a secret marriage between Bob Dylan and the Marquis de Sade" (*New York World Journal Tribune*). "One magnificent moment of hysteria," said *Fire Island News*, while *East Village Other* announced, "Art has come to the discotheque and it will never be the same again."

Long live the new flesh, trash, and heat. Watch out, the world's behind you. . .

"IF THE WHOLE THING WORKS OUT, IT WILL BE REALLY GLAMOROUS."
WARHOL

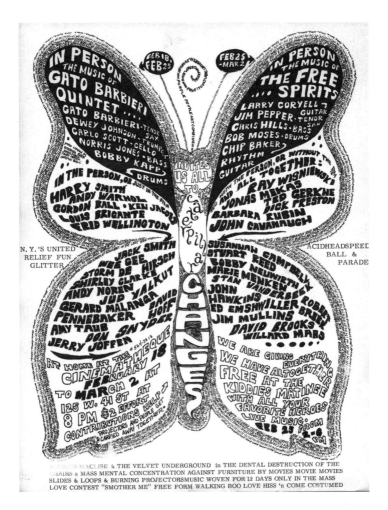

Poster for Barbara Rubin's "Caterpillar Changes" multimedia festival at the Filmmakers Cinematheque, New York, February–March 1967. "She was the moving force and co-ordinator between us all," said Reed.

5
RUN RUN RUN

The Velvet Underground & Nico: The Debut Album

Now it went bananas.

In a way, it began with Norman Dolph. It wasn't the only thing Norman did—in 1974 he wrote the words for the much-loved and much-loathed "Life Is a Rock (But the Radio Rolled Me)" which gave Reunion a Top Ten US pop hit, with its silly-smart, self-aware lyrics listing radio favorites from B. Bumble and the Stingers to Mott the Hoople, and from Wilson Pickett to Mungo Jerry. Sung by the guy (Joey Levine) who'd chirruped "Yummy, yummy, yummy, I Got Love In My Tummy" with The Ohio Express, it eulogized "Miracles in smoky places/slide guitars and Fender basses." Dolph worked with Isaac Hayes, Eddie Kendricks, Millie Jackson and KC and the Sunshine Band too. Yet, for all these glories, his place in popular music's history is assured by his helping to fund, and on some debatable levels produce, the first Velvet Underground record, now universally regarded as one of the most influential albums ever made.

Recorded hurriedly and in a piecemeal manner while the *Exploding Plastic Inevitable* tour was praised more for its spectacle than its music, it broke every rule of pop and rock and rewrote the vocabulary of sound. On top of that, Reed's lyrics dared to probe the murky nooks and crannies of the wild side: drugs, sex, and more drugs and weirder sex. The album's been credited with blowing the doors of perception off to the point where it invented, or at least made subsequently possible, punk, art rock, white noise, goth, indie, shoegazing, and a million Velvets copyists.

Routinely ranked high among any critics' poll of the greatest records ever created, it was inducted by the Library of Congress into the National Recording Registry in 2006. Initially a poor seller, it prompted the oft-repeated Brian Eno maxim of May 1982. Usually misquoted, Eno was primarily talking about himself when he told Kristine McKenna of the *Los Angeles Times* over the phone: "My reputation is far bigger than my sales. I was talking to Lou Reed the other day, and he said that the first Velvet Underground record sold only 30,000 copies in its first five years. Yet, that was an enormously important record for so many people. I think everyone who bought one of those 30,000 copies started a band! So I console myself in thinking that some things generate their rewards in second-hand ways."

Although it wasn't released until March 12, 1967, most of the tracks were recorded in mid-April '66, at Scepter Studios in Manhattan. Scepter Records had been founded in 1959 by producer and businesswoman Florence Greenberg, with the money she received upon selling Tiara Records and The Shirelles to Decca. (When The Shirelles failed to sustain their success at Decca, she happily took them back.) She oversaw hits for Tammi Terrell, Maxine Brown, The Kingsmen, and, most memorably, The Isley Brothers' "Twist and Shout." The offices moved to West 54th Street in '65, where the same building later housed, presumably to Warhol's delight, Studio 54. There was a small, run-down, 4-track recording studio there, in which not much of special note was achieved. Until now, when this incongruous group showed up. How on earth did they rock up there?

This is where Dolph, at the time a Columbia Records exec, came in. He'd DJ'd at a Warhol exhibition in Philadelphia, and the artist, wishing to promote the Velvets, asked him if he could handle such minor inconveniences as finding a studio, recording them, and getting them a deal. Dolph, something of a can-do entrepreneur, booked Scepter for three nights between April 18 and 23. Scepter had a competent engineer in John Licata, and Dolph contributed, though even he has said Reed and Cale made most of the decisions. He's said they had four days, which meant around three of recording and one of mixing, each "day" being a four-hour session; Moe Tucker has said it was eight hours total. This, costing in the region of $2,000, was all the band and Andy, who'd taken a recent financial hit which was almost entirely his own fault, could afford. Dolph chipped in some cash on top and received a Warhol painting as a trade-off. Warhol was stunned at how much recording studio time cost. He'd got used to making acclaimed alternative movies for a hundred dollars or so. One can imagine his face, blanker than ever, reacting with a silent wow to the mysteries and machinations of the music business.

Nonetheless, he's credited as the producer of this classic work. In truth, nobody was officially the producer—Dolph and Licata took care of the technical side; Reed and Cale bossed the musical choices. (We've yet to come to Tom Wilson's involvement.)

"I never felt I had the authority to pick takes, or veto them," Dolph says in Joe Harvard's *The Velvet Underground: The Velvet Underground & Nico*. "That, to me, was clearly up to Cale, Reed and Morrison. Lou Reed was more the one who'd say, 'This needs to be a little hotter'—he made decisions. And the mixing was really between Cale, Sterling and John Licata—that was all, again, done in real time." On the recording process itself, he adds, "From a take-wise point of view you weren't presented with many options. They either got it right, or broke down, or did a couple . . . it wasn't as though you got seventeen takes. Either you chose this one or chose that one, and then you went on and did the next. Usually they'd do a piece of one, then come in and listen to it. If one got largely through then broke down, they'd come in and listen and say, 'Yeah, that sounds like we got it right.'" Dolph described Warhol as sitting politely in the background. "He was more of a . . . presence, really."

On *The South Bank Show* in 1986, Lou Reed said, "The advantage of having Andy as a producer was that because he was Andy Warhol they left everything in its pure state. They'd say: is that alright Mr. Warhol? And he'd say . . . 'Oh! Yeah!' So, right at the beginning, we . . . record things our way and essentially have total freedom." Andy also insisted the "provocative" lyrics remain untamed. "I think Andy was interested in shocking, in giving people a jolt, and not let them talk us into taking that stuff out in the interest of radio play or popularity. He said, 'Oh you've got to make sure you leave the dirty words in.' He was adamant about that. He didn't want it cleaned up, and because he was there it wasn't." Nobody, Reed added, wanted it to sound "professional." "Andy doesn't know how to translate ideas into musical terms," Danny Fields said in Harvard's book. "He was making them sound like he knew they sounded at the Factory. The way it sounded to him when he first fell in love with it." In *Popism*, Warhol muses, "I was worried that it would all come out sounding too professional. One of the things that was so great about them was they always sounded so raw and crude. Raw and crude was the way I liked our movies to look, and there's a similarity between the sound in that album and the texture of *Chelsea Girls*, which came out at the same time."

In a 1989 interview with Bill Flanagan for *Musician*, Reed reminisced further. "Andy was in fact behind the board, gazing with fascination at all the blinking lights. He just made it possible for us to be ourselves and go right ahead with it. In a sense he really did produce it, because he was this umbrella that absorbed all the attacks when we weren't large enough to be attacked. As a consequence of him being the producer, we'd just walk in and set up and do what we always did and no-one would stop it because Andy was the producer. Of course he didn't know anything about record production, but he didn't have to. He just sat there and said, 'Oooooh that's fantastic.' And so the engineer would say, 'Oh yeah—right! It IS fantastic, isn't it?'"

Warhol was winging it just as blithely when it came to what to do with the record, once made. Half-hearted efforts were made to pitch it to labels like Atlantic and Elektra, but the controversial subject matter and the band's less than friendly image scared them off. Sterling Morrison reckoned they hated the sound of Cale's viola to boot. Enter Tom Wilson.

As crucial to this beautiful monster's birth as Dolph, Wilson was a thirty-something black record producer who'd blossomed at Columbia Records. He'd already worked with left-field jazz artists like Sun Ra and Cecil Taylor, then since joining Columbia had produced key Bob Dylan albums like *The Times They Are a-Changin'*, *Another Side of Bob Dylan*, and *Bringing It All Back Home*. When Dylan was asked by *Rolling Stone* if Wilson had given him his "gone electric" rock (as opposed to folk) sound, Dylan replied, "Did he say that? More power to him! He did to a certain extent. That is true. He had a sound in mind." Having helmed "Like a Rolling Stone," Wilson then reworked Simon & Garfunkel's "The Sound of Silence," famously adding drums and electric instruments to an acoustic track originally recorded in 1964 for the duo's debut album, *Wednesday Morning, 3 A.M.* The remix gave them their breakthrough hit.

The Velvets weren't exactly folk rock, but Wilson had recently signed The Mothers of Invention to Verve Records, producing *Freak Out!* Frank Zappa applauded his vision and willingness to stick his neck out. Most would have freaked out presented with the Velvets' first sessions, but Wilson, in the process of setting up a rock wing to complement MGM-owned Verve's jazz roots, not only loved what he heard but dangled the holy grail of a deal. He did, naturally, want to make some tweaks.

It was arranged that they would record further tracks in May '66, doing so at TTG Studios in Hollywood while on that otherwise ill-fated Californian trip. (The Mothers of Invention and The Animals, another Wilson act, had previously worked there.) In two days they got down "I'm Waiting for the Man," "Heroin," and "Venus in Furs." It's hard to imagine the album having the same impact without those additions. Wilson also wanted more Nico, so as nobody was rushing a release date, another session was booked in New York at Mayfair Studios, MGM again picking up the tab and Wilson producing. "Sunday Morning" was the result. The idea had been for Nico to sing it, but Reed was sternly sure he was the man for the job. There was ongoing tension between Nico and the men in the band. She would leave before the album's release, though Wilson, a loyal fan, would produce her solo debut.

Further tension was induced by that record deal, with Reed ensuring the payments went directly to the band and then paying Warhol his cut from that. (Reed, ever mercurial, also began saying Wilson was the "real" producer.) Warhol was wounded by this perceived betrayal: another factor in the imminent severing of bonds.

Personal niggles aside, surely everything was now looking rosy for the flowers of evil which constituted the record? The course of the Velvets never ran smooth. Delays continued as Verve got nervous about Reed's lyrical topics; problems were encountered producing Warhol's unconventional cover; and The Mothers of Invention's album had to come out first on the label, their own manager Herb Cohen being no shrinking violet. Warhol's famed passivity, and general cluelessness about the music business, didn't help here.

At last, in March '67, Verve didn't so much release the album as leak it. Two singles, "All Tomorrow's Parties" and "Sunday Morning," had preceded it, albeit without any kind of promotion. Neither was the album effectively hyped, even if the label did choose to highlight the Warhol name as the chief selling point, with ads shrieking of "the most underground album of all!" and "Andy Warhol's new hip trip to the subterranean scene." One ad inquired, "What happens when the daddy of Pop Art goes Pop Music?" It remains one of pop's great ironies that the record turned out to be, as history has evidenced, the ultimate slow burner. Such ads only gave people the impression that the group were a flash-in-the-pan joke, too clever by half. Reviews fixated on the grimy gutters of Reed's themes, believing them to be autobiographical as opposed to poetically observational, and assumed the band were 24-7 drug-hoovering kinky sex maniacs. Little wonder, then, that upon birth the album died a death, its journey into the world further hindered when Factory star Eric Emerson (*Chelsea Girls, Lonesome Cowboy*), desperately needing money after a drug bust, sued the label for its use of his image, among others, without his permission, on the back cover. As if the front wasn't controversial enough. (We'll curve back to the banana.) Verve reacted by recalling many copies of the album, placing black stickers over Emerson on more, and even reprinting further copies with Eric's face obscured. This took time, and hamstrung the record's distribution process yet again. (The original image was restored on a 1996 reissue.)

Eric went on to sing for the glam-punk band The Magic Tramps, one of the first to play CBGB in New York. He died in mysterious circumstances in 1975, aged twenty-nine. Debbie Harry, in the book *Making Tracks*, recalls his charisma, enigma, and demise. "One night we were over at Eric's apartment working on a tape of 'Heart of Glass' on his four-track tape recorder, when he suddenly staggered out of the kitchen looking ashen. He looked even more distraught and sad when we left. Being satisfied drove him crazy in the end—because he had everything he didn't care about anything anymore . . . the next day we were sitting around the house just after we woke up when Barbara (Winter, his partner, ex-wife of rocker Edgar Winter) called with the bad news. 'Oh, Eric got hit by a truck.'" (There emerged rumors, unsubstantiated, about a heroin overdose.) "He had been a good friend and inspiration to so many people," added Harry. "Eric's death definitely marked an end to the glitter period."

Back in 1967, the Velvets' debut was being banned from most radio stations and record stores. The underground hadn't crossed over yet. On May 13, the album entered the *Billboard* chart at No. 199, "peaking" after Verve's various false starts at No. 171. Yet as we all now know, and as Robert Christgau was to write in a 1977 *Village Voice* reappraisal, "It sounds intermittently crude, thin and pretentious at first—but it never stops getting better." As recently as 2012, *Rolling Stone* called it "the most prophetic album ever made." It's time we peeled off to engage with its eleven epochal tracks.

* * *

"Sunday Morning" may not sound overtly like a revolution, but the last song recorded for the album, their idea of a potential hit, opens it with a dreamy haze which both lulls you into a false sense of security and gently hints at undercurrents of unease. "It's just a restless feeling," sings Reed. And, "I've got a feeling I don't want to know." Cale contributes celesta, viola, and piano, having spotted the first instrument in the studio; Morrison's on bass, and Nico gently brings backing vocals to a song she'd previously sung lead on in shows.

Written at dawn after a Saturday night up partying, the song drew from Morrison the comment that it captures that feeling when "you're crawling home while people are going to church. The sun is up and you're like Dracula, hiding your eyes." Reed revealed to Victor Bockris in *Transformer: The Lou Reed Story* that Warhol had coaxed him into exploring its themes. "Andy said, 'Why don't you just make it a song about paranoia?' I thought that was great so I came up with, 'Watch out, the world's behind you, there's always someone watching you,' which I feel is the ultimate paranoid statement . . . in that the world cares enough to watch you." Yet the song's structurally pretty, and its sinister subtext is so subtle that many have since covered it with focus on its simple beauty. It's been interpreted a thousand ways, with versions recorded by everyone from Beck, James, Villagers, and Billy Bragg and Courtney Barnett to Orchestral Manoeuvres in the Dark, The Undertones, and Belle and Sebastian. Nico of course got to sing it herself later. And so a song specifically requested by Tom Wilson as a vehicle for her has become, thanks to Reed's stubbornness, something else entirely. The Velvets were multifaceted and wilfully unpredictable.

As is confirmed on what follows. "I'm Waiting for the Man" is one of the definitive garage rock anthems, a staccato, proto-punk, urban uppercut which drills into your psyche while forcing foot stomping. First worked up in a more folky, Dylanesque manner, the recording became a sonic encapsulation of the meaner streets and attendant hassles of New York. The piano and rhythm guitars chop relentlessly, attaining the state of a drone while never sacrificing raw energy, Tucker stays relentless, and Lou, dripping a sneery charisma, deadpans his seedy tale of trying to score heroin. Twenty-six dollars? "Everything about that song holds true," Reed insisted, "except the price." He also once wryly called it "a love song about a man and the subway." He'd actually first sketched it out while still in college, presumably influenced by favorite authors like Burroughs and Hubert Selby Jr., but it feels truly lived. And he did score drugs from Harlem. "The power of John Cale's piano . . ." wrote Reed in 2003. "I know how hard he was hitting it because I was there."

Along with "Heroin," it scandalized and drew both flak and attention. David Bowie, after his early manager Kenneth Pitt brought him back a copy from New York, fell in love with it and performed it loyally, over decades, throughout his career. The Stooges took a stab. Reed readdressed it solo, as did Cale, Nico, Tucker, and even Doug Yule (yet to enter the story). In December 2020, The National's front man, Matt Berninger, performed a rousing version of it on *The Tonight Show* with Jimmy Fallon. Fast, slow, or medium-paced, it retains its astonishing drive and drama. It's easy to comprehend why it was conceived as the album's opening statement until "Sunday Morning" dawned. It's the essence of the Velvets, a startling, stirring manifesto. A Harlem shuffle like none that had previously been heard.

"Femme Fatale" eases us back to a kind of tranquility, albeit typically troubled. Nico's voice strides forward in uniquely stentorian style. Lou had written it about Edie Sedgwick, at Warhol's request. "Don't you think she's a femme fatale, Lou?" he'd asked. Sterling Morrison later said that Nico hated her vocal. The song plays you for a fool if you fall for its surface beauty—the lyrics are of course laced with a nasty, bruised bitterness.

Nico reinterpreted it in 1982 with The Blue Orchids, and it's been covered by, among numerous others, R.E.M., Big Star, Tom Tom Club, Propaganda, Tracey Thorn, Duran Duran, Teenage Fanclub, Elvis Costello, Aloe Blacc, and The Slits.

If the resentment of Edie is veiled on "Femme Fatale," some vein of aggression is thoroughly candid on the paean to sadomasochism and fetishism which is "Venus in Furs." Reed had, as previously touched on, read Leopold von Sacher-Masoch's 1870 book. It had made a big impression on the young man, but again the lyrics aren't autobiographical per se—he essentially translates the book's story to verse. Cale's electric viola brings the intriguing, inventive atmosphere over five minutes plus which effectively invent "drone rock." Another factor in the off-kilter sound was Reed's guitar tuning, with, on one track, every string tuned to the same note (The so-called "Ostrich Tuning," see chapter 2). Morrison was again reluctantly on bass; Tucker playing bass drum and tambourine, not so much languidly as morbidly.

Morrison was later, in 1986, to tell Ignacio Julia: "That was completed before we met Andy," (he's referring to the writing, not the recording), "so it reinforced the associations with the book *The Velvet Underground*, as if in fact we were trying to make some statement about being S&M. That was wholly accidental. The book itself is incredibly stupid, about wife swapping and swingers in the suburbs and all that. We always did like the (band) name though; I still like it." Morrison, Reed, and Cale had recorded demos of it in their Ludlow Street loft, with Cale on lead vocal, prior to the very different album version, and had a stab at it in the Scepter sessions before the TTG version that swirls here. In an essay on the song, Erich Kuersten wrote, "The track starts as if you opened a door to a decadent Marrakesh S&M opium den, a blast of air-conditioned Middle Eastern menace with a plodding beat that's the missing link between (Ravel's) 'Bolero' and Led Zeppelin's 'When the Levee Breaks.'"

And so the tale of Severin, whipped by his demanding mistress Wanda (in furs), content to a degree to be her slave, became a pop song which few anticipated would be deemed a landmark over fifty years on. And though Reed smirked that everybody was dumb enough to think he invented masochism, the Factory's contemporaneous cinematic output certainly encouraged this link.

(In the film *Vinyl*, Gerard Malanga and Edie Sedgwick played out submissive/dominatrix roles.) Those "shiny, shiny, shiny boots of leather" were made for walking by Cale's avant-garde ear, and the song is one of the group's now-classic calling cards from the demimonde. For Morrison, it was as close as they ever came to perfectly realizing their vision, to "being exactly what I thought we could be."

Bowie, early Velvets adopter, was heavily inspired by the song for his 1967 track with The Riot Squad, "Toy Soldier." And speaking of *Vinyl*, "Venus in Furs" was covered by Julian Casablancas of The Strokes in the 2016 TV series of that name, in a scene referencing the Factory. As was "Run Run Run." Relatively conventional, or at least clearly recognizable as a Dylan-flavored rock 'n' roll piece, "Run Run Run" was reputedly written quickly on the back of an envelope, on the way to a gig, by Reed, who contributes a fierily effective, counterintuitive guitar solo. Those drug references run amok here, as fixes are sought or lost by gloriously named characters like Teenage Mary, Seasick Sarah, Beardless Harry, and Margarita Passion. The namechecks for Manhattan locations made what would have been mundane to locals seem glamorous to outsiders. Cale reverted to bass, Morrison to rhythm guitar, but this one is Reed's show: direct, unapologetic, pugnaciously poetic.

Our trip into the twisted gets magnificently melancholy again as "All Tomorrow's Parties" coaxes us into an enigmatic nocturnal mist. The Warhol crowd was an endless source of inspiration for Reed, and this was Andy's favorite offering from the band. Lou told David Fricke in 1995 that it was a "description of certain people at the Factory at the time . . . I watched Andy, and I watched him watching everybody. I would hear people say the most astonishing things, the craziest things, the funniest things, the saddest things." John Cale told *Uncut* in 2006 that the song "was about a girl called Darryl, a beautiful petite blonde with three kids, two of whom were taken away from her." (Darryl's fate also part-inspired Reed's *Berlin* album, as we'll discover later.) Cale's piano motif was somewhat motivated by listening to Terry Riley, who he'd worked with under La Monte Young. Reed's guitar tunes every string to D; Morrison's again on bass against his preferences. The Velvets were nothing if not perverse. Of course, Nico's vocal, double-tracked, is one of her most beloved and beguiling. Legend persists, determinedly despite contrary evidence, that it was written about her, or Edie.

Cut to half-length for the single, it inevitably did not bother any chart countdown. The song's title has become a signifier for a kind of vague wistful despair, appearing over the years as the name of a turn-of-the-century William Gibson cyberpunk novel and a now-defunct UK music festival, as well as numerous other items wishing to appear cool by association. It's a magnet for cover versions too, with gothic-infused interpretations coming from Bauhaus and Siouxsie and the Banshees, and other readings emanating from Bryan Ferry, Nick Cave and the Bad Seeds, Simple Minds, Buffalo Tom, Icehouse, and even Jeff Buckley. Surely the finest of all is that by Japan, who in 1979 recorded it for the album *Quiet Life*. Released (remixed) as a single four years later, it reached No. 38 in the UK, finally taking "All Tomorrow's Parties" into the hit parade.

If "All Tomorrow's Parties" is dark, the seven minutes of "Heroin" are darker. Interviewed for *What Goes On* by Phil Milstein in the eighties, Moe Tucker said, "'Heroin' is a mess . . . we didn't know what the hell we were doing, as you can hear from the record. We just didn't have the time. 'Heroin' drives me nuts. That's such a good song—I remember getting chills whenever we played it, and to listen to it on the album, it's really depressing. Especially to think of someone who listens to that and never heard us live . . . and they think that's 'Heroin,' and say, 'What's the big deal? It's a pile of garbage on the record.'" Warming to her theme, she discusses the "guys" being plugged straight into the board at the studio, and goes on, "Of course I couldn't hear anything. Anything. And when we got to the part where we speed up . . . I couldn't hear shit. I couldn't see Lou, to watch his mouth to see where he was in the song . . . so I stopped . . . and they just kept going. It's infuriating, because if you've seen us live, that's a bitch, that song. I consider that our greatest triumph."

Historically, more people have concurred with Moe that it was a triumph as opposed to a pile of garbage. Another written by Lou before he even came to New York, it does carry some autobiographical clout, as he was dabbling with the titular drug. He's said he was attempting some sort of exorcism in writing it, to push away his self-destructive urges, and not to—as is often assumed—celebrate heroin. It was neither for nor against, but a sensory description. As someone versed in literature, it baffled and irked him that it was seen as such a controversial, provocative topic in a song. Two chords (and no bass) and the truth. Although when the Velvets re-recorded the New York take in Hollywood, Reed tweaked the opening line from "I know just where I'm going" to "I don't know where I'm going," which Cale (whose electric viola again disturbs the rock format and its crescendos) and some hardcore heroin defenders perceived as a dilution.

"When I saw how people were responding to (the songs) it was disturbing," Reed told Lester Bangs in *Creem* in '71. "Because people would come up and say, 'I shot up to "Heroin," things like that. For a while, I was even thinking that some of my songs might have contributed to the consciousness of all these addictions and things going down with the kids today. But I don't think that anymore: it's really too awful a thing to consider." While covers have brazenly been recorded by such acts as Echo & The Bunnymen, Billy Idol, Roky Erikson, and Mazzy Star, perhaps the most applauded retake is Reed's own on his 1974 live album, *Rock 'n' Roll Animal.* Thirteen minutes long and featuring slick but brilliant guitar work from Steve Hunter and Dick Wagner, one feels Moe Tucker might have enjoyed it more than the one she played on. Many would disagree, as the Velvets' ramshackle energy scrambled music's maps. "Any band can play this," wrote Reed in the *NYC Man* compilation liner notes. "That's what I like about my songs. You can have the IQ of a turtle and play a Lou Reed song. It's really true. I love that about rock and roll." "If someone wasn't holding it down," said Tucker, "it would just be this mass of confusion. So I was there as something to come back to . . ."

"There She Goes Again" veers back toward the center of things, even aping a guitar lick from a 1962 Marvin Gaye release, "Hitch Hike." It's "normal" enough that R.E.M. covered it in '83. Yet there's always a tinny, ticklish oddness to the most conventional Velvets songs, even this jangling upbeat jaunt. As Sterling Morrison said in the Joe Harvard book, "Metronomically, we were a pretty accurate band. If we were speeding up or slowing down, it was by design. If you listen to the solo break (on this song), it slows down—slower and slower and slower. And then when it comes back into the 'bye bye byes,' it's double the original tempo. A tremendous leap to twice the speed." While the point with the Velvets is never even remotely whether they could "play" (in terms of conventional technical proficiency) or not, he wasn't wrong. They could play like the Velvets.

And Nico could only sing like Nico. "I'll Be Your Mirror" is her showcase, written specifically for her by Reed after, according to Victor Bockris's book *Transformer*, she intoned those four words to Lou at an early Velvets gig she attended. Recording it wasn't an easy process for her, as she repeatedly sang it more forcefully than in the soft, gentler attitude the band had envisaged. Recalled Sterling (in Bockris's book *Up-tight*), "She kept singing 'I'll Be Your Mirror' in her strident voice. Dissatisfied, we kept making her do it over and over again until she broke down and burst into tears. At that point, we said, 'Oh, try it just one more time and then fuck it—if it doesn't work this time we're not going to do the song.' Nico sat down and did it exactly right." On another occasion, more succinctly, Morrison offered that Nico was "just really depressed" that day. The band (and Warhol) remained fans of the song even after she left, and in the Doug Yule era he was still singing it with a dash of mimicry of her German accent. The Primitives, named after the early Reed/Cale band, covered it on their 1989 album *Pure*, and Shakespears Sister, and Susanna Hoffs are among others who've seen their reflection in its tender, folk-tinted contrast to the Velvets' more serrated forays. "Compassionate, very loving," Reed called it. "One of my favorite songs forever," he wrote in 2003. "A song of infinite desire," reckoned Cale.

One wouldn't use that phrase to describe "The Black Angel's Death Song," a pioneering, relentless slab of experimental psychedelic noise which began as a poem Lou penned at college. "The idea here was to string words together for the sheer fun of their sound, not for any particular meaning," he wrote in his later collected book of lyrics. Over a track which might have peeled the paint off the walls at Scepter, Cale's electric viola is given free rein to discombobulate, feedback abounds, and the Welshman hisses and growls into the microphone to create further disorientation and dissonance. Cale also played bass as Morrison, having been unhappily coerced to do so on "Venus in Furs," put his foot down and stayed on guitar along with Reed. The "song" owes more to Cale's avant-garde jazz and classical tastes than to rock, though its babbling bloodstream has informed rock ever since. "We played Tom Wilson this and 'Heroin,' screaming fucking loud with feedback, broke the speakers, all that shit," Cale told Allan Jones in *Uncut*. "And Tom goes, 'Yeah, hey, you're, er, creating something exceptionally good there.'"

It's notoriously the number which got the band axed from their Cafe Bizarre residency in '65: An incendiary version was too feral to handle for the manager, and when he asked them not to play it again they did so with twice the ferocity. A decade ahead of "punk."

If that wasn't goading and inflammatory enough, the album's closer is close to eight minutes of improvised distortion, feedback, and unnerving paranoia. "European Son" begins amicably enough with Reed singing Dylan-like tropes over a straight rock 'n' roll boogie format, but then an almighty crash (made by Cale picking up a metal chair and battering a pile of plates with it, causing glass to break) heralds the sea change. Then on, it's a shaking, quaking ocean of shock and awe. It hints at sounds, or even anti-music, which the group were to explore on the next album. Tucker has stated the unsurprising: that it turned out differently every time they tried it. Lou dedicated it to his writing mentor Delmore Schwartz, who was not a rock fan, which has added poignancy given Schwartz died three months after its April recording. Poignant because it's bitter rather than sentimental. Reed addresses his near-hero, who'd become increasingly reclusive as his life force ebbed away, with reproach for not letting him visit. "You made your wallpaper green . . . your clowns bid you goodbye." Ultimately, though, "European Son" isn't about the words; it's a watershed in intended, warped, noise. An assault on the expected. "We wanted to break the rules," Cale told Allan Jones. "So we broke every fucking rule we could." "There was no structure, we just did it," recalled Moe Tucker to Phil Milstein in *What Goes On*. "The engineer, my God, he's saying, 'What are you DOING?' But . . . it was tremendous."

It's not the kind of thing a sensible person tries to "cover," though Thurston Moore has bravely given it a bash, as has Gary Lucas. Holger Czukay's bassline on Can's "Father Cannot Yell" emulates Cale's somewhat. And Japan and Simple Minds have both released their own songs borrowing its title.

In the summer of peace and love, *The Velvet Underground & Nico* was completely out of step and out of this world. The delays in its release, more cock-up than conspiracy, hadn't helped at all. And that Warhol cover, now recognized as one of the all-time greats, had held back its emergence even longer. It remains today his most iconic record jacket, though as mentioned earlier he'd worked on many album covers for jazz and Blue Note's captains of cool.

He had plenty of ideas as to how to dress his new toys. One was to feature a set of images of plastic surgery: nose-jobs et al.

Eventually, he settled on his bright yellow silk-screened banana which he conceptualized as a sticker. When you peeled the yellow banana, underneath was a pink one. Plenty of Warholian sex-related suggestiveness there. Inevitably, printing such a complicated cover and sticker set-up took time and money, and the absence of the band's name from the design confused and misdirected. Only the artist's signature appeared, leading many to believe it was an album by him. MGM, who'd paid for it, weren't entirely averse to this misconception, given the Warhol name's heat. Another ad read, ". . . featuring Andy's Velvet Underground (they play funny instruments). Plus his this year's Pop Girl, Nico (she sings, groovy). So far underground you get the bends!"

All in all, the marketing of one of the definitive rock albums was a complete debacle. In later decades, the album was reappraised and rehabilitated, and reissued many times. Bands queued up to claim its influence and gain credibility by connection, and critics eulogized its genius. In July 2006, *The Observer* placed it at No. 1 in a list of 50 Albums That Changed Music, and eleven years later *Pitchfork* hailed it as the best album of the sixties, no less.

Yet at the time, the mess initiated Reed and Warhol parting ways, and Nico floating away from the mothership into her own space. The loyal Tom Wilson kept the faith, sticking around for the next album, 1968's *White Light/White Heat*. The Velvets had only been with Warhol a year or so. Much, history has shown, had been achieved, but right now everybody was fraught and frustrated. Nico drifted to her beloved Ibiza again for modeling work, then London via Paris. When she re-materialized in the US, she came along to a Velvets gig in Boston, expecting to sing with them. But according to most reports, her lateness meant they'd already played "her" songs, and they refused to let her join them onstage. The honeymoon, such as it was, was over. Warhol sided with her but she disappeared again. It wasn't like she had nothing else interesting to do, reviving an affair with The Doors' singer, Jim Morrison, in L.A., before eventually coming back to New York to play solo gigs at the Dom, with helpful guitarists including on separate occasions Reed and Cale (amicably enough), Tim Buckley, Tim Hardin, and Jackson Browne. She began recording her *Chelsea Girls* album with Tom Wilson and, confusingly, various Velvets. But she was solo now; her role in the band was over. They were happier doing their own thing; they'd always felt she'd been imposed upon them by Andy. "To me, she was just a pain in the ass," said Moe Tucker bluntly.

The breakup with Andy made a sad kind of sense. Each party had sucked growth and media attention from the association and, to be less cynical, inspiration. In late summer, though, Lou decided new sensations were needed, as well as some semblance of good business sense regarding the music industry, never Warhol's forte. Ironically, it was Andy kindly suggesting Lou think about a career plan which prompted Lou to do so. So Lou left his "manager," assuming the band was with him. "So I thought about it—and I fired him. He did not try to stop me, legally or otherwise," he said. "He did, however, tell me that I was a rat. I think it was the worst word he could think of." John Cale seems to have been kept in the dark a little. Many years on, he shrugged, "I thought Andy quit." Both Reed and Cale perceived Andy more fondly after his death, their rose-tinted reminiscences informing their 1990 album, *Songs for Drella.*

Steve Sesnick came in as their new manager, to Cale's displeasure, and sure enough it wasn't long before tensions were rife again. And yet now they cohered to make a second album which blazed with shared incentives. Sterling Morrison was quoted in a 2013 *Mojo* article as remembering that "We were all pulling in the same direction. We may have been dragging each other off a cliff, but we were all definitely going in the same direction."

THE VELVET UNDERGROUND & NICO

RECORDED
April–May and November
1966, at Scepter, New York, NY;
TTG, Hollywood, CA; Mayfair,
New York, NY

RELEASED
March 12, 1967

LABEL
Verve

PRODUCER
Andy Warhol, Tom Wilson

PERSONNEL
Lou Reed (lead vocals, backing
vocals, lead guitar, sound effects);
John Cale (electric viola, piano,
bass guitar, backing vocals, celesta,
hissing, sound effects); Sterling
Morrison (rhythm guitar, lead
guitar, bass guitar, backing vocals);
Maureen Tucker (percussion,
drums); Nico (lead vocals on
"Femme Fatale," "All Tomorrow's
Parties," and "I'll Be Your Mirror,"
backing vocals)

TRACK LIST
All songs written by Lou Reed,
except where noted

SIDE ONE
Sunday Morning (Reed, John Cale)
I'm Waiting for the Man
Femme Fatale
Venus in Furs
Run Run Run
All Tomorrow's Parties

SIDE TWO
Heroin
There She Goes Again
I'll Be Your Mirror
The Black Angel's Death Song
   (Reed, Cale)
European Son (Reed,
Cale, Sterling Morrison,
   Maureen Tucker)

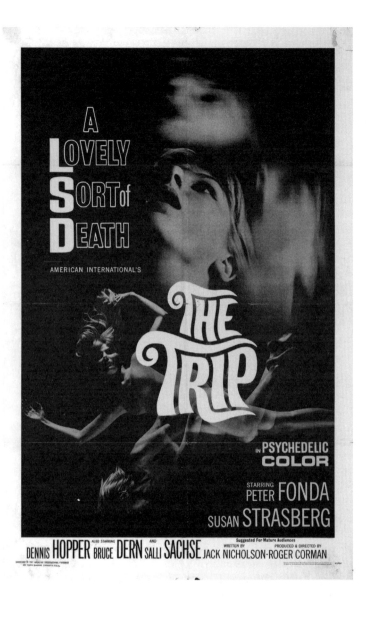

Poster for Roger Corman's film *The Trip*, 1967: The Velvets, a tough act to follow, opened two Boston screenings of this counterculture classic/folly.

6
WHITE HEAT

Licking their wounds after the commercial failure of that debut album, The Velvet Underground toured their hard-to-sell noise, improvising with increased abandon, through most of 1967—the year they split from Nico and Warhol. They returned to Scepter Studios for just two days to record their second album, and it was released in January '68. "The Statue of Liberty of Punk," Lou Reed later called it. "A grimy, unflinching album," wrote *Record Collector*'s Oregano Rathbone in 2013, discussing a 45th anniversary reissue. "Its blunt prescience simply can't be eroded, however often it's been replicated or ripped off."

The Velvets–Warhol period, relatively brief as it was, has of course left a still-burning legacy, as much by accident as design. Moe Tucker, interviewed by Phil Milstein for issue 4 of *What Goes On*, was laconic about the drifting apart. Asked when and how Nico left, she said, "You're asking the wrong person. I really don't remember." Pushed harder, she conceded that she thought Nico left when the *Exploding Plastic Inevitable* shows ended. And why did those shows end?

"I guess Andy got bored with it, and we wanted to make records and be a group. I don't think either he or us ever entered into it as a five-year proposition. It was something fun to do . . . and as we got into it, it became more fun and more interesting. But then we had other interests, and so did he. So we parted all the best of friends."

According to Moe, they had no trouble getting plenty of gigs straight away thereafter. She vaguely suggests that this was down to their new manager, much as she's reluctant to give him credit. A Boston-based club owner with the gift of the gab and some elementary financial savvy, Steve Sesnick was deemed necessary by, in particular, Reed. Asked how he came onto the scene, Tucker's memory improves.

"Sesnick was in California when we were at the Dom. Andy knew him somehow, and when Andy found us, he called him and said, 'I have a band,' and Sesnick set up jobs in California. After he heard us and decided we had something, he started thinking more about just being our manager. He made sure he kept in touch with us, so that when we did want to have a manager, he'd be there." Recalling that there was "another guy" who wanted to manage them, Tucker can't remember his name but, "I hate to say it, and I hope Steve doesn't read this, but we might have been better off with him. Simply because he wouldn't have been our friend. But we wanted Sesnick because he was more our type of person. The other guy was too 'businessy,' y'know?"

Lou had pushed for Sesnick. Cale wasn't keen and felt he caused disharmony by fawning over Lou and perceiving him as the front man. Both Reed and Cale spoke nastily of him in later years. Right now, he was getting them booked at shows where they were playing pretty much what they wanted to play, and this scored him points. He gave them regular dates at his club The Boston Tea Party (one Jonathan Richman was a recurring face in the audience, becoming a zealous fan—he claims to have seen them over a hundred times, and later supported them). And in October '67 they were the opening act for a weekend of Boston screenings of *The Trip*,

Streetlight fancies: the VU plus friends during the shoot of Piero Heliczer's *Venus In Furs* film, New York, November 1965.

Reflect what you are in case you don't know: Cale and Reed at Café Bizarre, New York, December 1965.

Femme fatale: Nico and Sterling onstage at the New York Society for Clinical Psychiatry annual dinner, The Delmonico Hotel, New York, 13 January 1966.

What goes on: at the Velvets' show at a "Freakout" party at the Action House, Island Park, Long Island, New York, stargazers included (L to R) Paul Morrissey, Nico, Andy Warhol, Gerard Malanga.

The gift: Reed, Morrison, Cale and Tucker pose with the second album in 1969.

From out on the island: Warhol superstar Candy Darling appearing in the play *Vain Victory: The Vicissitudes Of The Damned* in 1971.

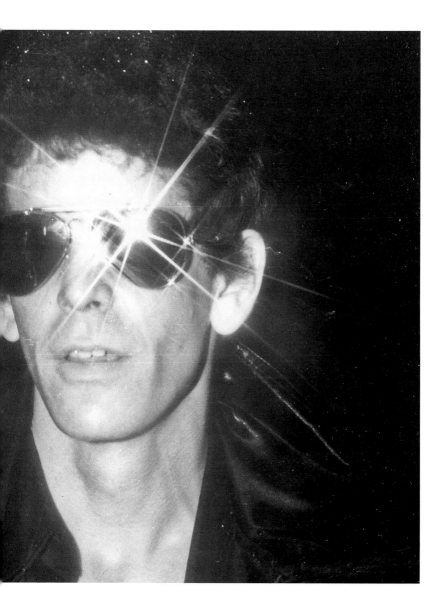

I'm not gonna wear my heart on my sleeve: Lou post-Velvets, circa "Street Hassle".

New Age: Doug Yule, Willie Alexander, Mo Tucker, Walter Powers identify as The Velvets in Hilversum, Holland, 11 October 1971.

After Ziggy broke up the band: Lou, Mick Jagger, David Bowie and Lulu at Bowie's aftershow, Café Royal, London, 7 April 1973.

Taking no prisoners: Lou live at L'Olympia Bruno Coquatrix, Paris, France, 25 May 1974.

Some kinda love: The Velvets reformed play Ahoy, Rotterdam, 9 June 1993 (L to R: Cale, Tucker, Reed, Morrison).

Shakin' to that fine fine music: The Rock'n'Roll Hall Of Fame inducts the band, 1996
(L to R: Tucker, Sterling Morrison's widow Martha, Cale, Reed).

After hours: Lou with avant-garde artist and future wife Laurie Anderson, performing in The Hague, Netherlands, 12 November 2003.

the psychedelic Roger Corman acid casualty of a counterculture, sex-and-hallucinations movie starring *Easy Rider*'s Peter Fonda (and written by his partner in LSD lore, Jack Nicholson; Dennis Hopper and Bruce Dern also featured).

Sesnick also—ambitiously—tried a charm offensive on Beatles manager Brian Epstein, hoping to finesse a deal for the band's songs with his publishing company. Surprisingly, Epstein didn't instantly laugh him out of town, but he died before rumors of him helping the Velvets with a European tour could be substantiated. Sesnick did succeed in getting MGM/Verve to fund the band's touring costs, which was a big leap forward from Warhol's foggy efforts. With no other income, they gigged hard, though only ever, at least in this era, in America. It's fascinating to imagine a scenario where Michelangelo Antonioni flew them to Swinging London to appear in his 1966 Cannes Grand Prix-winning film *Blow-Up*, but the Italian director, having considered it, realized it would be too expensive, and pragmatically went with local boys The Yardbirds instead.

For all this productivity, Cale increasingly felt Sesnick was more concerned with Reed's career than the band's, seeing him as the front man, songwriter, and potential star. Morrison was dubious about the money matters, and Tucker came to feel he was overly zealous, visualizing them as an overground crossover and rejecting alternative paths they should have taken. And by now, Cale was in a relationship with "youthquake" fashion designer Betsey Johnson, who he was to marry in '68. She'd been a contemporary of Lou and Sterling at Syracuse University. Edie Sedgwick became her in-house model. Reed felt a little left out, perhaps intimidated by the fact that Johnson was a very forthright personality. To further cloud the issue, she'd briefly dated Sterling previously. Once again, even without Nico, the band's internal relationships were tense, and chafed.

Arguably, this helped them create the assault on the senses that was *White Light/White Heat*. "We were free to pursue anything we wanted," said Morrison. Although, as he said, they were all (mostly) pulling in the same direction when they made it, you can hear the music itself pulling all conventional wisdom apart. It desperately wants to burst its banks, and does. "Troublesome" was a word Cale used when formulating his manifesto for the music, while he and Reed argued non-stop about their choices, sometimes opting for throwing punches instead of verbal barbs. Their own marriage of convenience was approaching its end, with Cale thinking about leaving already. Reed was acting more unpredictably than ever, with Morrison saying that Lou's mood swings switched, depending on his drug intake, from "boyishly charming" to "vicious." Tucker just thought the whole lot of them were insane, and tried to stay out of the flare-ups. "Uncontrollable personalities," said Morrison.

Somehow, or perhaps inevitably, they concocted this uncontrollable record. "It's a very rabid record," offered Cale in the *Peel Slowly and See* liner notes in 1995. "The first one had some gentility, some beauty. The second one was consciously anti-beauty." The Summer of Love? Hippie flower power? Trampled underfoot, stems mashed. Hit sideways.

And yet, at the same time, and for the first time, a terrible beauty is born.

Those trips to the West Coast had only inspired the Velvets to react against the prevailing tides. While Sterling emphasized that they "had good table manners and paid our hotel bills—we didn't smash up any furniture," and talked of their "middle-class upbringings," they loathed the hippie peace-and-love vibrations which flowed in San Francisco and its environs. Not enough paranoia, not enough ugliness, not enough dirt. In Victor Bockris and Gerard Malanga's *Up-tight*, Sterling phrased it thus: "Inspired by media hype and encouraged by deceitful songs on the radio— Jefferson Airplane, The Mamas & Papas—teenage ninnies flocked from Middle America out to the coast. So, at the height of this 'Summer of Love,' we stayed in NYC and recorded *White Light/ White Heat*, an orgasm of our own." Lou Reed in 1987 told *Rolling Stone*, "There were a lot of casualties. It wasn't funny anymore. I don't think a lot of people realized at the time what they were playing with. That flower-power thing eventually crumbled as a result of drug casualties . . . it was a nice idea but not a very realistic one. What the Velvets were talking about, though it seemed like a down, was just a realistic portrayal of certain things." On *The South Bank Show* in '86, he'd said, "I was trying to give you a shot of the street."

So in just those two September 1967 days they again trashed the template and made this abrasive, bracing, unlikely landmark. A "difficult second album," yes, but redefining "difficult" in all the most exhilarating ways. The melodies and surface sweetness which had infiltrated the aggression of the debut were parked as they doubled down on bark and bite. Feedback in overdrive, lyrics which shocked the unshockable, it blitzed into new terrain in both sound and subjects. It also featured a cantaloupe.

"White Light/White Heat," a live regular now, was released as a single the same month as the album's emergence, with "Here She Comes Now" as the B-side. As the album's opening, the very first second lets you know you're not in Kansas anymore, racing in jaggedly as if its head's been lopped off. It isn't just about a methamphetamine rush: It is one. That barreling piano from Cale, Reed clipping out the lead vocal while Cale and Morrison chime in on the title refrain, the fuzzy-as-fun guitars, Cale taking us out and up and down with the treated bass outro, Tucker banging away with customary simple effectiveness: The track is relentless yet also refreshing. Yet amid its giddy twitching it carries the foreboding of the post-high descent . . .

And while, yes of course, it's about speed, the Factory's drug of choice, Reed in a radio interview in 1969 sold it as having deeper, more metaphysical themes. One never knows whether he was, as was his wont, winding up the interviewer (in this case Portland Oregon's KVAN Radio), but he suggested a more cerebral reading. "I've been interested in what they call 'white light' for a long time," he drawled, referencing his studies of a Japanese healing method which is "a way of giving off white light." He added that one can "call down a stream of pure white light," citing a book named *A Treatise on White Magic* by Alice Bailey, which he described as "incredible."

That said, the song's afterlife and myriad cover versions have tapped into its adrenalized rush. Glam, punk, and metal are indebted to this ultra-urban blues. The Velvets' live versions extended it from its under three minutes here to, for example, nine minutes on *1969: The Velvet Underground Live* album. Reed himself went on to play it alongside everyone from David Bowie (in '72) to Metallica, while Bowie's inhabiting of the song as Ziggy Stardust helped nail his aura. He included it in his live show from '71, and "Queen Bitch" on *Hunky Dory* credits it as inspiration. It at last made it onto one

WHITE LIGHT/ WHITE HEAT

RECORDED
September 1967, at Scepter,
New York, NY

RELEASED
January 30, 1968

LABEL
Verve

PRODUCER
Tom Wilson

PERSONNEL
Lou Reed (lead vocals, lead guitar,
rhythm guitar, cantaloupe); John
Cale (lead vocals on "The Gift,"
backing vocals, electric viola,
Vox Continental organ, piano,
bass guitar, medical sound effects);
Sterling Morrison (lead guitar,
rhythm guitar, bass guitar, backing
vocals, medical sound effects);
Maureen Tucker (percussion,
drums)

TRACK LIST
All songs written by Lou Reed,
except where noted

SIDE ONE
White Light/White Heat
The Gift (Reed, Sterling Morrison,
    John Cale, Maureen Tucker)
Lady Godiva's Operation
Here She Comes Now
    (Reed, Morrison, Cale)

SIDE TWO
I Heard Her Call My Name
Sister Ray (Reed, Morrison,
    Cale, Tucker)

of his albums on the *Ziggy Stardust: The Motion Picture* live album, and he returned to it many times. It was only rock 'n' roll, but unlike it. San Francisco radio stations banned it.

Then we're given "The Gift," which isn't what anybody expected. It begins with Waldo Jeffers having reached his limit, but from there on, for eight minutes, denies the existence of limits. Until it ends with a macabre, accidental stabbing. Humor doesn't get much blacker.

Reed had written a short story in his Syracuse creative writing class, motivated by a summer of long-distance yearning, separated from early girlfriend Shelley Albin (a relationship which was to spark on and off, preoccupying him for years). He told Lester Bangs in *Creem*, "I wrote 'The Gift' while I was at college. I used to write lots of short stories, especially humorous pieces like that. One night Cale and I were sitting around and he said, 'Let's put one of those stories to music.'"

In said story, Waldo pines for Marsha Bronson. Cale narrates this tale in his distinctive Welsh burr, Tucker hitting her ritualistic patterns, Reed and Morrison on guitars, Cale also playing an ominously fuzzed-up bass. Fidgeting in the knowingly named Locust, Pennsylvania, Waldo becomes increasingly paranoid that Marsha won't stay faithful and true. Our zealously jealous guy can't afford a ticket to travel to Wisconsin to see her, and so decides to mail himself to her in a big cardboard box. "It was absurdly simple." He thinks she'll be delighted to see him. He's shipped out Friday; arrives Monday. Marsha's having a chat with a friend about the guy she canoodled with over the weekend—"like an octopus—hands all over the place!"—as Waldo waits for his box to be opened. It's a tussle to open it, until Marsha hands her friend a sheet metal cutter, which the friend then unwittingly plunges into Waldo's head. As it splits open, his head sends "little rhythmic arcs of red to pulsate gently in the morning sun."

While there are echoes of Poe, the story's genuinely well written; its arch, cynical tone just the right side of dry. Yet its marriage with the music gives it near-mythical dimensions. Cale recites superbly (he did it in one take), finding the fusion of deadpan and dramatic. He's mixed through one speaker, the music responding through the other. David Fricke has reported (though some have disputed it) that that mesmerizing music had been worked out by the band members in live shows as an instrumental going by the name "Booker T." (They seem to have thought it resembled Booker T. & the M.G.'s' classic groover "Green Onions.") And then there's the cantaloupe.

How to approximate the sound of poor, doomed, loser-in-love Waldo getting his head caved in in the name of romance? At the suggestion of Frank Zappa, whose Mothers of Invention were working at the same studio, Lou reckoned that bashing a cantaloupe with a wrench (or just stabbing it manically, according to others' recollections) would cover that. He was reportedly disappointed that in the end his melon-based musical efforts didn't come across more loudly on the track.

The Velvets revisited it in their nineties reunion, but perhaps its larger legacy has been to enlighten, through its darkness, the fact that spoken word and music together could be thrilling and cinematic. Its influence can be traced informing work by innumerable art house bands since, from Blue Aeroplanes to The Clientele to Alphabet Saints. The presence of "The Gift" keeps on giving.

"Lady Godiva's Operation" is no less unsettling, covering what *Rolling Stone* pragmatically called "botched medical procedures." Cale (his electric viola once more crucial) again takes vocals, at least at first, and, foreshadowing his own later solo work, it's clear he's a very charismatic singer. Reed, who wrote the song, comes in midway, the clash of tones deliberate and telling. There's a deception, a misdirection, as Cale sings of Godiva (it's debatable whether she bears relation to the naked horseback rider of Coventry legend) before Reed blurts in with a sick and twisted description of the operation, where "ether caused the body to wither and writhe . . . doctor arrives with knife and baggage, sees the growth as just so much cabbage." It's rather Gothic (and we'll present the case for the Velvets' significant influence on "Goth" further on). Cale opens his toy box of sound effects and has a grisly ball. He's credited with "medical instrument vocal noises," as is Morrison. Was this chiller brought on by Reed recalling the electroshock treatment he'd suffered as a youth? Perhaps. He sometimes suggested so. Others have jumped to conclusions that the track is referring to sex-change operations, but this seems understandably colored by linking everything the Velvets did with some of Warhol's films and early themes. Either way, the Summer of Love would have run away sobbing, its feelings hurt.

"Here She Comes Now" arrives as what appears to be a respite; a simple, shimmering song, just two minutes of calm, giving the iconoclasm a rest. It had been written originally as a vehicle for Nico, in the "Femme Fatale" style, and she'd sung it live a few times. Reed's chippy phrasing propels it along succinctly. Of course, it's not without its provocations. Radio stations banned the single for perceived sexual content. As Reed told *Time Out* in 1972, "We put out 'Here She

Comes Now' in San Francisco and they said, 'That's about a girl coming.' And I said, 'Well no, it's not, it's about somebody coming into a room.' And then I listened to the record and I realized it probably WAS about a girl coming, as a matter of fact. But then again, so what? But we were banned again." Others more innocently theorize that it's about Lou's guitar—"ooh, she's made out of wood"—and back this up by pointing out his frequent whoops, in various performances, of "here she comes now" before a guitar solo. There's a balm to this brief cut which enhances the album's overall drama, and it feels like a trailer for much of Reed's seventies solo output. Nirvana, Galaxie 500, Cabaret Voltaire, and others covered it. It keeps on coming.

"I Heard Her Call My Name" is the yin to its yang. Loud, pugnacious, and heated, its not one but two Reed guitar solos are astonishingly visceral, while the feedback sprays break the meter. Morrison hated it, telling Victor Bockris in *Up-tight* that "I quit the group for a couple of days because I thought they chose the wrong mix for 'I Heard Her Call My Name,' one of our best songs that was completely ruined in the studio." Yet Reed reckoned his shredding was a tribute to Ornette Coleman, the jazz saxophonist he greatly admired. As he told David Fricke in 1989, "There were two sides of the coin for me—R&B, doo-wop, rockabilly; and then Ornette Coleman and Don Cherry, Archie Shepp." Mentioning his college radio show, *Excursions on a Wobbly Rail*, he adds, "I used to run around the Village following Ornette Coleman wherever he played." So to his ears the almost deranged solo in "I Heard Her Call My Name" was honoring free jazz. "I wanted to play like that. I used the distortion to connect the notes, so you didn't hear me hesitating or thinking. I never thought of it as violent. I thought it was amazing fun." Incalculably influential, on generations of unconventional guitarists, as was the unbridled energy of the track in general.

"I like to think of Sister Ray as a transvestite smack dealer," Reed once said, ensuring—as does this one-take seventeen-minutes-plus landmark in rock's creativity—that we climax big. Ding dong. It's an improvised jam driving away under Reed's tawdry tale of drag queens and their attempts to have an orgy meeting with frustration. Searching for their mainline. Couldn't hit it sideways. Lester Bangs wrote in his book *Psychotic Reactions and Carburetor Dung*, "The early Velvets had the good sense to realize that whatever your capabilities, music with a simple base was the best. Thus, 'Sister Ray' evolved from a most basic funk riff into seventeen minutes of stark sound structures of incredible complexity."

The longest piece the band recorded in a studio is credited to all four members, with Reed's lyrics—now typically—touching on said themes: drug abuse, violence, homosexuality, and transvestism. In *Up-tight*, he says, "'Sister Ray' was done as a joke . . . no, not as a joke, but it has eight characters in it and this guy gets killed and nobody does anything. It was built around this story that I wrote about this scene of total debauchery and decay. The situation is a bunch of drag queens taking some sailors home with them, shooting up on smack and having this orgy . . . but the police appear." The influence of one of his literary heroes, Hubert Selby Jr., is again evident. He also said (on Tom Robinson's 6 Music radio show), rather surprisingly, that Ray was named as a tip of the cap to The Kinks' front man, Ray Davies.

On another occasion (*Rolling Stone*, 1989) he recalled that Warhol had insisted, "Oh Lou, make sure that you do the sucking-on-my-ding-dong song." The bell for the opening round having rung, they decided to accept whatever occurred in that one improvised take, without exception. The guitars are Reed and Morrison, while Cale goes berserk on an organ fed through a guitar amp and much distortion. There's no bass. In the *Lou Reed: Rock and Roll Heart* documentary, Reed reports that engineer Gary Kellgren left the studio while the track was recorded, saying, "I don't have to listen to this. I'll put it in record, and then I'm leaving. When you're done, hit that button and come get me." In Anthony DeCurtis's *Lou Reed: A Life*, he embellishes the anecdote with Kellgren saying, "You can't pay me enough to listen to this crap. I'll be down in the commissary getting coffee." "That's completely true," Reed insisted.

Cale's organ blasts and honks away irrepressibly, sometimes with a dash of ? and the Mysterians, sometimes decidedly Doors or Seeds, more often just its own wild beast. Everyone veers off-piste, by design, with Moe Tucker just about holding the center. It's Ornette Coleman, it's punk, it's heavy metal, it's garage rock if the garage hadn't been cleaned in an aeon.

Tucker has confided that Tom Wilson was not at his most diligent on the day. He "was more interested in the blondes running through the studio," she told *What Goes On*. "Witness the forte song 'Sister Ray,' where he forgot to turn on the damn mics. Better than the first album, but that part there drives me crazy." Cale has also said that Wilson's attention and focus had wandered. "He knew more, er, ladies of the night than there are women on this planet," he told *Creem* in 1987. "He's a swinger par excellence. It was unbelievable—a constant parade into that studio." And yet this couldn't have happened without Wilson's say-so. "He was inspired, though," added

Cale. "He used to joke around to keep everybody light." Considering the Velvets' tensions, that was probably no small task.

Sterling said Cale was so loud on "Sister Ray" that he couldn't hear his own guitar. It's as if the four knew the best way to avoid arguments was simply to blast the thing out mercilessly, competing with each other, trying to outdo each other's most feral emissions. It's as if it's their last anti-hurrah, their last chance saloon. Let it all out.

"'Sister Ray' succeeds because I don't think anybody can perceive it in any other way than it is," Sterling told Ignacio Julia. "But we intended it to be a lot cleaner and crisper, so even that was a disappointment. We were happy that something like that was on the record, but for the whole album we anticipated a much better sound, something that would just fly out at you. And that didn't happen. In fact all our efforts to make it happen were ironic—it made just the opposite happen. The louder we played in the studio, the quieter they had to do the mastering. Nobody was pleased with that, but there was nothing to be done." He later added, discussing the album as a whole, "Still though, as a record, it has its own little place in the rock pantheon. It did accomplish something: maybe warned other groups—avoid these excesses. I'm not embarrassed by it. I just wish it could have come out a whole lot better. I like the songs."

The legacy of "Sister Ray" can't be overstated. Its name has been taken by record shops and bands, it's been covered by Joy Division and New Order, by Suicide and The Sisters of Mercy. The Stooges sucked it up; it trickled down to Nirvana. Fanboy Jonathan Richman's track named "The Velvet Underground" swerves into a section of it, and his calling-card hit "Roadrunner" (organ solo by its producer—John Cale) is like a more upbeat, Pollyanna-ish photocopy. Buzzcocks formed after Howard Devoto placed an ad looking for musicians to play "Sister Ray" with him. More overarching is the fact that every band since that has elected to spiral in and out and up and down from a two- or three-chord baseline has ingested "Sister Ray" with gusto. And in the poetic waking-dream life of rock, it may not be too fanciful or tenuous to wonder if Bowie would've sung, on "Breaking Glass" on *Low*, "Don't look at the carpet, I drew something awful on it," if he'd never heard and loved *Sister Ray*'s line "Don't you know you'll stain the carpet?"

It's almost needless to point out that the *White Light/White Heat* album stalled at a heroic No. 199 on the *Billboard* Top 200 (in March '68), before belatedly becoming, like its predecessor, a monumental icon. We have British amplifier manufacturers Vox to thank for some of its murky sound, as the Velvets had recently, implausibly, signed an endorsement deal with them. The British Invasion—by The Beatles, the Stones, The Who, The Kinks, and others—had made Vox amps and instruments cool in America. The Velvets were an unlikely ally to promote their equipment, but didn't hold back in experimenting by, essentially, turning everything up to eleven and firing up the fuzz pedals. "We played them emphatically," said Morrison, presumably in a wry tone.

The question remained of how to wrap this gift. How do you follow a time-consuming, distribution-destroying, work-of-art Warhol banana? Well, with a little help from Warhol, as it turned out. By now, he and the band had vented their wrath sufficiently to revive a decent rapport, and it was Andy who suggested Billy Name as the answer. As Lou wrote in a letter to Gerard Malanga in December '67, Warhol recommended using "a black-on-black picture of a motorcyclist tattoo by Billy. Beautiful. ALL BLACK!" The skull tattoo under consideration had already appeared in Warhol's film *Bike Boy*, on the bicep of its star Joe Spencer. So Billy Name further claimed his stake in Velvets lore, enlarging a black-and-white still from the film—Reed has claimed he chose which one—and layering it against a night-black background. In all honesty, it fails on every "correct" artistic or commercial design level. You have to strain, or hold it under the light, to realize it's not merely a plain black cover. On the back is a bleached-out, technically poor band shot by Mario Anniballi. Again, rules ignored, new rules invented. It was the nihilistic antithesis to the era's flower power and psychedelic rainbow-colors, the same year as *Sgt. Pepper*, which had been released six months before. To bastardize the lyrics of that, the Velvets weren't guaranteed to raise a smile. But they were certainly a thrill.

So next, what goes on? Cale is set free . . .

"THERE WERE A LOT OF CASUALTIES. IT WASN'T FUNNY ANYMORE. I DON'T THINK A LOT OF PEOPLE REALIZED AT THE TIME WHAT THEY WERE PLAYING WITH."

LOU REED

Cool it down: the Yule, Morrison, Tucker and Reed line-up, May 1969.

7
WHAT GOES ON: LOU TAKES (SOME KINDA) CONTROL

"It was undisciplined art," said John Cale in 2018 at a Broadway exhibition called *The Velvet Underground Experience*. "It was very energetic and frivolous and enjoyable." Pondering the cleaner, less chaotic New York of today, he offered: "It's a little alien. It's like I'm looking at a replica. I didn't mind the grime so much in the sixties. It was really fodder—it pushed us in one direction to really get something done."

His own Velvet Underground experience was, in September 1968, about to end (at least until the nineties reunion), just four years after he'd co-founded the band. He and Lou Reed were now at near-constant loggerheads, although somewhat typically, the manipulative Reed coerced Sterling Morrison, who didn't want Cale out at all, into breaking the news of the split to the Welshman. "Lou always got other people to do his dirty work for him," Cale sighed later.

Reed, distracted and fascinated by his on-off affair with Shelley Albin, called Morrison and Moe Tucker to a meeting at the Riviera cafe in Greenwich Village. Cale must go, he'd decided. Morrison gave his opinion: such a move was "unthinkable." Reed declared that if Cale didn't go, the band was completely over. Morrison and Tucker didn't want that, so chose what they saw as the lesser of two evils.

Sterling spoke at length about the breakup to Spanish interviewer Ignacio Julia in 1986. He began by revealing that he was surprised by Lou's animosity toward John at that point: In the wake of *White Light/White Heat* he thought they were having "good times." "I don't remember any reason really being given . . . some general statement that he couldn't stand playing with John any more for umpteen inexpressible reasons." He added that Cale was playing brilliantly at gigs and that, now "running around with Betsey Johnson," he was "very well-dressed and responsible, doing fine." So, surmised Sterling, "maybe Lou got jealous. Something like that." If so, it wouldn't be the only time a nominal front man became envious of the musical sidekick's glamorous life: Some allege Bryan Ferry resented Brian Eno's dalliances with ladies in the early days of Roxy Music, for example. But, as Sterling went on, John was no more hard work than anyone else among the band's egos. Moe would, when there was craziness, just "watch it work itself out." So Sterling thought himself "in the Cale faction. John was my roommate on the road and as often as not in Manhattan. After he was kicked out I still hung around with him. The whole business speaks very badly for me, because I should have quit or at least called (Lou's) bluff. It was Lou's scheme, and he gets the blame for it, but I get the blame for complicity. I thought it much easier to go along being The Velvet Underground than being nothing by siding with John. I don't think I displayed good character in all of that. I couldn't convince Lou. All of it had a kind of unreal quality—it was like discussing your own funeral arrangements." As for musical differences, "We had them from the first minute we were in a room together—but that made the band good."

If Sterling beat himself up about it, Lou focused on the larger popular success he envisaged. Cale certainly had pushed experimentation, and Sterling thought Lou was now "maybe more in a pop direction. Lou always wanted to get there if he could; he only had to figure out how. It's tough to be a pop success." The Velvets' last studio session with Cale in '68 involved three Reed pop-orientated songs—"Stephanie Says," "Temptation Inside Your Heart," and "Beginning to See the Light"—and just one Cale-initiated, viola-heavy drone, in "Hey Mr. Rain."

After playing his last gig with the band later that month at the Boston Tea Party, Cale departed with a measure of dignity, declining to kick up a fuss. "We were barely able to be in the same room for five minutes by the time we recorded *White Light/White Heat,*" he reminisced in *Uncut* in 2013. "Lou was getting more satisfaction from writing pretty songs and wanted to go in that direction. And he had an ally in Steve Sesnick, the manager, who went to Moe and Sterling and said, 'Look, this is Lou's band. You are the backing band. That's the way it's going to be.' It was only a matter of time before word got around to me." Sesnick, sneered Cale, "wanted us to . . . sell shirts. He knew somebody who was making frilly shirts, so he thought we could go and promote these for him. No, none of us wore the shirts."

In later years, Reed would come to agree that they'd split too soon. Right now, the ongoing friendship between John and Sterling only fueled his ever-present paranoid tendencies. Tucker conceded that something was lost from the band, and that something, she said, was "lunacy." Cale, of course, went on to innumerable great things. His replacement in the group was, ironically, first discovered by Morrison, though Reed very much liked his malleable freshness.

The oft-maligned Doug Yule has arguably taken more stick than any substitute player in the history of rock. Very little of what he's blamed for was his fault. His chief crime was, essentially, not being John Cale. "Doug can play, he's a good guy," Sterling Morrison told Julia. "The only problem with Doug was . . . he was not John."

Like Lenny Bruce, Yule hailed from Mineola, Long Island, growing up in Great Neck. Born in 1947, he took music lessons as a kid, then studied acting at Boston University, before leaving after a year to play with bands including The Grass Menagerie. He'd seen the Velvets play at a student gig at Harvard in early '68, and later that year when they played the Boston Tea Party they crashed at his apartment—which he was renting from their tour manager Hans Onsager, a close associate of Sesnick's—on River Street. Morrison heard him practicing guitar, and commented positively to Reed. Chinese whispers ensued, and soon Sesnick was on the phone to Yule inviting him to New York for a chat. He arrived at Max's Kansas City for this chat in October '68, anticipating being asked to join in for future gigs, but was immediately asked to play bass and organ and offer some vocals, often standing in at the microphone for Lou, who was frequently, given his lifestyle, under the weather. He played his first gig with them that weekend. Touring continued with the amended lineup, and they promptly returned to TTG Studios—now renamed Sunset Highland Sound—in LA to record the third album through November and early December, while gigging at the Whiskey in the evenings. It was, in the main, the polar opposite to their second.

By mid-December, they were back in Boston, sharing the bill at the Tea Party with MC5. Their audiences were increasing

THE VELVET UNDERGROUND

RECORDED
November–December 1968,
at TTG, Hollywood, CA

RELEASED
March 1969

LABEL
MGM

PRODUCER
The Velvet Underground

PERSONNEL
Lou Reed (lead and rhythm guitar, piano, lead vocals except where noted, verse co-vocals on "The Murder Mystery"); Doug Yule (bass guitar, organ, lead vocals on "Candy Says," chorus co-vocals on "Jesus" and "The Murder Mystery," backing vocals); Sterling Morrison (rhythm and lead guitar, verse co-vocals on "The Murder Mystery," backing vocals); Maureen Tucker (percussion, lead vocals on "After Hours," chorus co-vocals on "The Murder Mystery," backing vocals)

TRACK LIST
All songs written by Lou Reed

SIDE ONE
Candy Says
What Goes On
Some Kinda Love
Pale Blue Eyes
Jesus

SIDE TWO
Beginning to See the Light
I'm Set Free
That's the Story of My Life
The Murder Mystery
After Hours

in number. Nineteen-sixty-nine saw a new phase in the Velvets' evolution. "After the glamour died down," Danny Fields has said, "it was Lou Reed and a back-up band. It was like any other rock group on the road." For some, Sesnick's influence had defanged them. (MGM registered them as an MGM band, rather than a Verve one, and injected some modest financial support.) "Their charisma was so strong," said Sesnick, "that no matter what they did it was accepted."

Charisma is not lacking on that third album, except for in its title: *The Velvet Underground.* (Some refer to it as "The Gray Album," with respect to the cover rather than its contents.) In every other way, it's highly distinct: restrained, subtle, and rich in love ballads and linear rock songs. While this is usually attributed to Reed pursuing his new direction, Morrison has pointed out the impact of their "gizmos" and "electronic bag of tricks" being stolen at the airport when they were on their way to the sessions. (Yule has since said that this is nonsense: The equipment could easily have been replaced.) "Rather than try to replace them, we thought about what we could do without them," said Sterling. "We never made fixed plans about what we'd do in the studio . . . I think our mood overall doing the third album was subdued for some reason or other, maybe because of the Cale thing. So even if not by design, that's the way it came out."

The Velvet Underground, released in March 1969, won surprisingly positive reviews, or was ignored. Reed claimed credit for the switch in style. "I really didn't think we should make another *White Light/White Heat,*" he's quoted as saying in Peter Hogan's book *The Rough Guide to the Velvet Underground.* "I thought that would be a terrible mistake, I really believed that. I thought we had to demonstrate the other side of us. Otherwise we would become this one-dimensional thing, and that had to be avoided at all costs." Morrison described his role in the project as "acquiescent." Tucker spoke of a "new calmness" within the group, of how they were looking to "a good future," actively wooing record companies. And the new boy, Yule, described the sessions as "a lot of fun . . . constructive, happy and creative—everybody was working together." The results included some of the most now canonical of Velvets moments, from "Pale Blue Eyes," to "What Goes On." They were, perhaps, beginning to see the light(er) side of things.

"Candy Says" opens the record: In late 2013, Reed was to sing it at what became his last ever public performance, and caught in the right mood he'd call it one of his best compositions. It's generally thought to reference Factory star Candy Darling—who reappeared in "Walk on the Wild Side"—and her wish to be free from her birth gender. In Anthony DeCurtis's *Lou Reed: A Life*, Reed emphasized its larger, less specific resonance, as being "about something more profound and universal, a universal feeling I think all of us have at some point. We look in the mirror and we don't like what we see . . . I don't know a person alive who doesn't feel that way." Reed had overworked his voice at shows, and Doug Yule sang it here. "Lou asked me, and I said sure," he told *Pop Matters* years later. "He was singing every song and he wanted to get away from that. He was trying to shift a little focus away from him too . . ." Much as Yule's voice can often sound similar to Reed's, Lou's own tones are easily recognizable on "What Goes On," which then raises the tempo, and became the album's only single (as well as the title of the band's appreciation society's fanzine, which was launched in 1978). An insistent, insinuating rocker, with multiple guitars from Reed and Morrison and a phrase ("lady be good") borrowed from the Gershwins, it's been covered many times, most notably by Bryan Ferry on *The Bride Stripped Bare*.

The melodic "Some Kinda Love" reminds us that the Velvets are here to pray rather than party. "Between thought and expression lies a lifetime," sings Lou, and the first four words were used as the title of both his book of collected lyrics and his anthology box set in the early nineties. In a live context he jokingly described the song as "a dialogue between a guy called Tom and a woman called Marguerita, and he's just trying to drink her like tequila and she doesn't like salt being thrown over her shoulder." (A pinch of salt is indeed what's required here: Reed also had a famed tendency to introduce Yule as his brother.) In "no kinds of love are better than others," the lyric encapsulates a recurring, bittersweet theme of its writer.

"Pale Blue Eyes" taps into that bittersweet vein even more poignantly and powerfully. According to Victor Bockris's book *Transformer* it was inspired by Shelley Albin, his married lover ("the fact that you are married . . ."). In the lyric book *Between Thought and Expression*, Reed wrote that it was actually sparked by a person with hazel eyes. Its beauty has long since transcended the nature of its birth, as its frailty and vulnerability—"thought of you as everything I've had but couldn't keep"—as well as Reed's brittle, bruised vocal, have established it as a classic of longing. It's been revisited by Patti Smith, Edwyn Collins and Paul Quinn, Hole, Counting Crows, R.E.M., and countless other fans of its elegance, as well as featuring in films as varied as *The Diving Bell and the*

Butterfly and *Adventureland.* Moe Tucker's 1989 version, with Reed on guitar, was its writer's favorite. In 2003 he wrote of the song (in the *NYC Man* liner notes), "It was pretty good to do this in '68 and Sweet Jane in '69, don't you think?"

"Jesus" landed on the B-side to "What Goes On," and it's so innocently devout that you peer for a typically subversive Reed twist. Yet it seems sincere, or at any rate faux-sincere, hands clasped, genuflecting. "The hopeful warmth at the center of the Velvets' rage," wrote David Fricke in *Rolling Stone*. "How do you define a group like this, who moved from Heroin to Jesus in two short years?" yelled Lester Bangs. "Can this be that same bunch of junkie-faggot-sadomasochist-speed-freaks who roared their anger and their pain in storms of screaming feedback and words spat out like strings of epithets? Yes, yes, it can, and this is perhaps the most important lesson of the Velvet Underground: the power of the human soul to transcend its darker levels."

The boisterous "Beginning to See the Light" takes this positivity and channels it into a joyful energetic rush (let's give Yule's bass some credit), while "I'm Set Free" is equally unembarrassed by genuine emotion. "That's the Story of My Life" is an incongruous yet concise detour into warped music hall, quoting the cryptic wisdom of Billy Name (who took the album's cover shots), but then we come to the true curveball, "The Murder Mystery."

On this nine-minute trip we're hauled back to the hypnotic Hades of earlier Velvets experiments. During the verses, Reed and Morrison recite stream of consciousness poetry (written by Reed) simultaneously, their voices panned left and right, and in the choruses (as such), Tucker and Yule (whose organ sets the tone, as the music theoretically holds the center together) sing different words and tunes, also positioned left and right. Does it work as intended? Debatable. Even Reed acknowledged that, "you couldn't hear either one well enough to hear what was being said." Is it fascinating? Without a doubt. Reed was trying to ascertain "if you could cause two opposing emotions to occur at the same time." What he possibly hadn't realized then was that The Velvet Underground's great gift was that they did that almost all the time.

"After Hours" takes us out into the wee small solitary sadness of existence, with Tucker, unusually, singing (her debut). Reed had thought her disingenuous, innocent take would lend it an extra quality. "It's a terribly sad song ... people wouldn't believe me if I sang it," he's quoted as saying in Peter Hogan's book. Moe was so nervous that she only let Lou and the engineer stick around while she gave it her best. "I was surprised that it was decent," she commented later. It's a suitable, spectral ending to an against-the-odds great album, somehow both soothing and unsettling.

It's one of the tracks that differs most in the fabled varied mixes of the album. There was MGM/Verve engineer Val Valentin's mix; the most commonly known. Then there was the alternative mix Reed did, pumping up his own voice and guitar contributions while dampening everybody else. Sterling referred to this as "the Closet Mix," deeming its sound akin to that of something recorded in a closet. This wasn't an insult—he thought it was "flat," "quiet," and "insane," adding in *Uptight*, "and that's the way we wanted it." There was also a mono mix, Tucker's favorite. (All three mixes have appeared on deluxe reissues in later eras.) The Reed and Valentin mixes feature different takes of "Some Kinda Love."

Billy Name's grainy, gloomy cover photos tell an accidental story. Snapped at the Factory, with the band sitting on the much-mythologized couch, the front shows Maureen and Doug gazing at apparent focal point Lou, who with an uncharacteristic smile holds an issue of *Harper's Bazaar* magazine. Sterling, closest to camera, looks off to the side, as if disinterested. "It was very nonchalant," said Name. On the back, it's just Lou, holding a cigarette, albeit his image is refracted as if in a hall of mirrors. "Lou at sort of his worst . . . would have temper tantrums and everyone would walk on eggs, tiptoeing around him or you would crack the shells," Billy told *Rolling Stone* in 2014. "That was really him. But then there are other memories of when he would just walk up and give me a hug. I just adored that. He was such a good friend and would often show me his natural love . . . that's how I prefer to think of him."

The *Village Voice*'s Robert Christgau praised the album, bar "The Murder Mystery," which he deemed "questionable." In fact it was among his top ten of the year. Lester Bangs in *Rolling Stone* preferred *White Light/White Heat*, but sacrificed credibility by calling "Pale Blue Eyes" a misstep. He did spin around to hailing the album's "brilliance." Naturally, it didn't sell at the time, waiting until 1985 to stagger to a dizzying No. 197 in the *Billboard* Top 200. It has of course starred strongly in innumerable lists of all-time greats in more recent years. Linger on . . .

"I'm sort of fond of almost everything on the album," mused Doug Yule to *Rolling Stone* in 2014. "And it's funny, cos . . . it just happened."

* * *

Through 1969, the Velvets persevered, playing shows and recording again: The tracks from and around the "lost" album made at New York's Record Plant emerged in the mid-eighties on *VU* and *Another View*. But their rapport with MGM was now sticky and the band weren't displeased, given the shoddy promotion on the third and previous records, when MGM let them go. The company president, Mike Curb, was short on enthusiasm as he bemoaned in a statement, "Groups that are associated with hard drugs . . . are very undependable."

"We owed them a record and we just wanted to be done with it," recalled Tucker, speaking to *Rolling Stone*, of the "lost" material. "We weren't being lackadaisical, or not trying to do our best, but in our minds it wasn't going to be released. Certainly not by MGM."

Gigs in Dallas and San Francisco in October and November yielded the double album *1969: The Velvet Underground Live*, which Mercury was to release from the vaults in '74. We'll wheel back to "posthumous" albums further on. Right now, the Velvets, as a group, were still just about alive, even if it took them several months to land another deal with a label. This one, hysterically, wanted hits. It wanted an album loaded with them.

"HOW DO YOU DEFINE A GROUP LIKE THIS, WHO MOVED FROM HEROIN TO JESUS IN TWO SHORT YEARS?"

LESTER BANGS

FOUND IN ALL THE NICEST HOMES

'Bon Goût' by David Goard (the well-known fraud).

THE VELVET UNDERGROUND

Loaded. (also available on Musicassette)

The Velvet Underground & Nico.

The Velvet Underground.

White Light/White Heat.

Andy Warhol's Velvet Underground featuring Nico. (double album)

MGM

MARKETED BY POLYDOR

There she goes again: 1970 Australian newspaper ad for the re-releases.

8
DIFFERENT TIMES: LOADED THEN SQUEEZED

Cotillion Records was a subsidiary of Atlantic, active from 1968 to 1985. Originally conceived as the mother label's wing for blues and soul, it had a brief fling with a scattergun approach before settling into success in its mature years with Sister Sledge, Slave, Stacy Lattisaw, and The Fatback Band. Along the way it dallied with Screaming Lord Sutch and Emerson Lake & Palmer. Yet with all due respect to the aforementioned purveyors of classy funk and disco, Cotillion is perhaps best remembered by history for releasing the fourth, and most purists would argue final, Velvet Underground album, November 1970's *Loaded*.

Atlantic, run by Ahmet Ertegun, signing the Velvets for two albums, insisted there must be no overt druggy references. We were entering a new decade. They also required an album loaded with hits, and we can all wonder at how broadly Lou Reed smirked behind his shades at the sly double entendre of the title: For the more prim and innocent among you, "loaded" can also mean "high on drugs." Doug Yule told the Velvet Underground fanzine *What Goes On* in 1994: "On *Loaded* there was a big push to produce a hit single. There was that mentality: which one of these is a single, how does it sound when we cut it down to three-and-a-half minutes? So that was a major topic for the group at that point. And I think that album to a great extent shows that . . . You can hear the derivation, like: this is a sort of Phil Spector-ish song, or this is that type of person song . . ."

"We delivered them *Loaded*, which is a very good album," Sterling Morrison told Ignacio Julia. "I liked it, Lou liked it while we were making it, track-by-track we were very happy." Yet again, it wasn't promoted or distributed well, according to Sterling. "We were so furious with Ahmet . . . we were mad, we had this great album that was going no place . . . worse than MGM, which we never would have thought possible." Ertegun insisted they should tour more. They felt they'd toured plenty, and went skiing for the winter. They refused to record a second album for him, so he released a live tape he'd bought from Brigid Polk for $2,000—*Live at Max's Kansas City.* "That record should only be understood as an attempt (by him) to punish us," asserted Sterling. "If I want to hear rotten sounding tapes, there's enough of those around."

Loaded came first, though, and if it was in some ways perverse that the band didn't record the songs from the so-called "lost" album (except for "Rock & Roll"), it did prove that they were confident and believed a fresh chapter beckoned. Or at least that some of them were. This was, to a degree, the Lou and Doug project, their passing musical bromance still in productive mode. Sterling was less involved in the daily pressures and politics, and had enrolled in further academic courses at City College of New York, partly perhaps to spend less time with Lou's tantrums, while Maureen Tucker, though credited, wasn't part of the recording at all. Maternity leave isn't a phrase one instantly associates with the Velvets' mythology, but her pregnancy meant that drums were mostly handled by Doug and his younger brother, Billy Yule ("a high school senior!" Moe laughed in chagrined disbelief), with drums on three tracks played by either engineer Adrian Barber or session player Tommy Castagnaro. "*Loaded* didn't have Maureen on it, and that's a lot of people's favorite Velvet Underground album," Lou Reed told David Fricke. "So we can't get too lost in the mystique of The Velvet Underground. It's still called a Velvet Underground album, but what it really is is something else."

Tucker's daughter Kerry was born in June. (She went on to have five kids in total.) Steve Sesnick was too impatient to let the others wait for her to come back. Doug Yule himself has questioned the wisdom of that, and Tucker was very irritated. "I personally, during the last year of the band, became generally depressed," she told *What Goes On*. "Because there was all of this crap, and they couldn't get along." No fan of Doug, she went on: "We would have liked a return of some kind."

In the next century, she told *Rolling Stone* that "I loved Lou very much. We had almost a brother and sister relationship. I saw him every few years (afterwards), and it was always nice. I loved all of the members of the band very much like brothers, and worried about them and was happy when anything good happened to them."

Part scapegoat, part the man who kept it afloat, Doug recalled (also in *Rolling Stone*): "Lou was a fanatic about loyalty. If you showed any disloyalty at all, he would react pretty strongly and, depending on what he was doing pharmacologically at that point, the reaction could be really violent . . . or just mildly violent." Tellingly, poignantly, he added: "We were never 'close' friends—not like Maureen was with him."

So exit Tucker, enter Yule, and for now the honeymoon was working. "I'm not on it—I wish I had been," Moe told *What Goes On*.

From April to August of '70, Reed and Yule, with intermittent Morrison input, laced up *Loaded* at Atlantic's New York studios, with production credits shared between the band and Geoff Haslam and Shel Kagan, who came in after engineer Barber had helmed the early sessions. But implosion inched closer again: Before its release, even Lou had left the band. And you know the pattern by now: An album sniffed and sneered at in its day is now revered as an all-time great. Doug is one of the most patronized musicians in rock lore, but he played bass, keyboards, guitars, and drums (if needed) here, as well as singing four tracks. And it probably wouldn't have got made without him.

"Sterling was kind of pissed off during it, which I didn't know until it was about three quarters over," he told *Rolling Stone*. "He felt that the group was being hijacked by me and Lou and he was being left out. But I think what was really happening was Steve Sesnick was pushing for hits and Lou was responding to him. So I was really naïve. I was just so happy to be in the studio and doing stuff that I just wanted to do everything all at once." He also suggested that recording in New York was a mistake as they all lived in separate places and "assembling" was less like a band and more like "going to work."

"Lou was a force of nature," Yule expressed to *Rolling Stone*. "He was an extremely strong-willed person. At the same time he could be an overbearing tyrant and a warm, fuzzy, puppy-loving person. He just . . . he was a human being."

Thus, the (to most minds) "last" Velvets album saw all ten songs credited to Reed . . . eventually. At first they went to the band: He snarled and made sure that was rectified. He also hated the original cover's lineup listings, with Doug coming first, then Sterling, then himself third, just before Moe. His other gripes? Just the mix, the edit, and the sequencing. A bridge cut from "Sweet Jane." Yet Yule has said (to Pat Thomas in 1995) that a disingenuous Reed had edited it himself, as keen as anyone else—if not more so—to create hooks and hits. Sterling moaned that he would have preferred Lou to sing all the tracks—even though it was Reed who asked Doug to bail him out when his voice was shot and his psyche was troubled. And Yule—who Reed then had the gall to criticize for not understanding the lyrics he sang—certainly often took care of awkward but essential things like arrangements. Surely, even the most anti-Yule, they-were-nothing-without-Cale Velvets aficionado has to love his guitar solos on "Rock & Roll" and "Oh! Sweet Nuthin'."

That cover art is adored by some, sneered at by others. Stanislaw Zagorski was one of the first Polish graphic artists to achieve acclaim and profile in the States. A founder of the Polish School of Posters, he delivered album covers for Otis Redding, Aretha Franklin, Miles Davis, and Cream, among others, but his *Loaded* work remains the most truly iconic. The Times Square subway station entrance depicted emits a purple haze of dubious constitution, somehow both psychedelic and dirty. Also, it's the underground! With something sort of velvet-ish creeping out of it, possibly malodorously! Given you're on a hiding to nothing replacing Warhol, and some have sniped that it's too literal, it's actually a triumph, and certainly more alluring and enigmatic than Billy Name's Velvets covers, uncompromising as those might be.

"*Loaded* had so many great songs on it," wrote Reed in 2003. The opening three songs were recently hailed by *Paste* as "among the best three-song openings on any rock and roll record," and while "Who Loves the Sun" is a bordering-on-country-rock jewel ("bouncy," said Lenny Kaye in his *Rolling Stone* review), it's "Sweet Jane" which has achieved anthem status. Reed was—of course— dissatisfied with this version, and went on to adapt it for decades in his own live sets. The missing bridge reappeared swiftly on the Max's album. Doug Yule reckoned the famed riff was nailed only shortly before recording. Its simplicity is rampantly effective, and it's become a staple, revisited by everyone from Mott the Hoople on the *All the Young Dudes* album (produced by Bowie) to Cowboy Junkies, who found a hushed beauty within its soul on 1988's *The Trinity Session*: Reed's on record as saying this was his favorite version. Even in 2020, Miley Cyrus covered it on *MTV Unplugged*. A signifier of alternative cool (like so many Velvets tracks), it's not going away.

"Rock & Roll" is equally starred in the Velvets' canon. Although its lead character is Janey, whose life—"despite all the computations"—is saved by the rock 'n' roll she hears on the radio, in the 1995 *Peel Slowly and See* box set Reed wrote, "It's about me. If I hadn't heard rock and roll on the radio, I would have had no idea there was life on this planet. Which would have been devastating— to think that everything everywhere was like it was where I came from. That would have been profoundly discouraging. Movies didn't do it for me. TV didn't do it for me. It was the radio that did it." It's another song he repeatedly returned to live.

"Cool It Down," with a dash of blues, thought Lenny Kaye, "quotes admirably from Lee Dorsey's 'Workin' in a Coalmine.'" "New Age" is sung by Doug (though Reed sang it live) and is probably another one inspired by Shelley Albin, though in its

LOADED

RECORDED
April–August 1970, at Atlantic,
New York, NY

RELEASED
November 15, 1970

LABEL
Cotillion

PRODUCER
Geoff Haslam, Shel Kagan, The
Velvet Underground

PERSONNEL
Lou Reed (vocals, rhythm guitar,
piano); Doug Yule (bass guitar,
piano, organ, lead guitar, acoustic
guitar, drums, percussion, backing
vocals, lead vocals on "Who Loves
the Sun," "New Age," "Lonesome
Cowboy Bill," and "Oh! Sweet
Nuthin'"); Sterling Morrison (lead
and rhythm guitars, possible
backing vocals); Maureen Tucker
(drums: credited on the original
album, but does not appear due
to maternity leave; on the *Fully
Loaded* edition, does appear
singing on the out-take "I'm
Sticking with You" and playing
drums on the demo of "I Found

a Reason"); Adrian Barber
(drums on "Who Loves the Sun");
Tommy Castagnaro (drums on
"Cool It Down" and "Head Held
High"); Billy Yule (drums on
"Lonesome Cowboy Bill" and
"Oh! Sweet Nuthin'")

TRACK LIST
All songs written by Lou Reed

SIDE ONE
Who Loves the Sun
Sweet Jane
Rock & Roll
Cool It Down
New Age

SIDE TWO
Head Held High
Lonesome Cowboy Bill
I Found a Reason
Train Round the Bend
Oh! Sweet Nuthin'

original draft the line "it seems to be my fancy to make it with Frank and Nancy" reverts to Factory-era tropes and hints at Reed's own bisexuality. This studio version was changed to a tale of a fan, or weirdo, semi-stalking a "fat blonde actress." It's somehow both sarcastic and romantic, a trick Reed was to master on his seventies solo work. The upbeat "Head Held High" makes you want to shout along, and "Lonesome Cowboy Bill," observed Kaye, "deserves a hallowed place on your favorite AM station." He pointed out that the candid, sweet "I Found a Reason" recalled, tangentially, Reed's fifties doo-wop ballad tastes: "what comes is better than what came before," wrote Reed in optimistic mode. The so-so "Train Round the Bend" showed a harder, blues edge again, while "Oh! Sweet Nuthin'" transports us out as an outlier, drifting across seven-and-a-half minutes after all these shorter, would-be hits. A hazy loll of harmonies and counterintuitively effective guitar by Yule, with its typically existential Reed lyrics it's one of the group's most underrated creations. If this is considered the last track on the last "proper" Velvets album, it's a pretty good way to go.

"When push comes to shove," wrote Tim Sommer in *The Observer* in 2015, "*Loaded* is a Velvet Underground album for people who don't especially like the Velvet Underground, for those who thought the first album was too fuzzy and night-cultured, the second too much of an ecstatic roar, and the third too hushed and holy."

Back at the time of its release, Lenny Kaye, who later would work with John Cale on Patti Smith's *Horses*, wrote: "Although on *Loaded* they're more loose and straightforward than we've yet seen them, there is an undercurrent to the album that makes it more than a mere collection of good-time cuts. Lou Reed's music has always concerned itself with the problem of salvation, whether it be through drugs and decadence or pseudo-religious symbolism. Now, however, it's as if he's decided to come on back where he most belongs . . . each cut, regardless of its other merits, is first and foremost a celebration of the spirit of rock 'n' roll, all pounded home as straight as an arrow." Elsewhere, Robert Christgau hailed it as "genuinely rock and roll" but also "really intellectual and ironic." It's also, as many have pointed out, a very enjoyable pop album, even if it wasn't, in the real world, "loaded with hits."

And yet it was Lou's farewell. The Velvets' nine-week residency at Max's Kansas City (from June 24 to August 28), with two sets each night, was thrilling but exhausting, somewhat like the related live album (released in 1972). Reed grew ever more tense and troubled, felt frustration at the lack of commercial progress, and was no longer even remotely enamored of Sesnick. During the final week of the Max's shows, he decided to quit. He'd told Moe Tucker, who was in the audience, but Yule was only informed by Sesnick an hour before the following night's gig that Reed wasn't turning up—"I thought he was late." Reed then professed surprise that *Loaded* was nonetheless released in November. "I left them to their album of hits that I made," he drawled. At least those Max's shows had caught fire. Lenny Kaye again, writing in *Rolling Stone*: "I would say without exaggeration that the music contained on [the Max's album tapes] is some of the finest rock 'n' roll that has been played in many a year. On a small stage, surrounded by a mass of dancing bodies, the Velvets fulfilled all of their early promise, taking even those classics which they had put aside for so long (such as "Heroin" and "Sunday Morning") and turning them out in somehow newer, brighter clothes. It was a homecoming, in more ways than one, and few who were there will soon forget it." This can be interpreted as high praise for the constantly criticized Yule brothers. And yet the sixties were now gone. And the sixties' arch nemeses, the Velvets, were effectively over too. "Reed has always been the focal point of the group; the one who wrote their songs and provided their magic," added Kaye (a comment which might potentially have caused awkwardness with Cale a few years on). He then prophesied: "And it is doubtful whether they can overcome his loss."

"The band split up right after I had Kerry," Tucker told *What Goes On*. "She was born in June 1970, and the band split up in August . . . still, today, it infuriates me that Lou left. I don't know if he just wanted to be on his own, or didn't want certain people around him. He never said to me, 'Well, here's the problem.' Maybe he didn't really know himself . . ." On other occasions she's blamed Yule, and Sesnick's enthusiasm for him. Sterling has said Reed kicked the drugs but was in poor mental shape: Shelley Albin was now pregnant by her husband and had left Lou once and for all. Lou talked of not sleeping, even of levitating; he raged at Sesnick—"he destroyed it and made it so it wasn't fun anymore." Despite the heroic buzz of the Max's shows (and that live album, Reed's last night and swansong on 23 August), Lou sighed, "I was not doing what I believed in, and it made me sick."

He was so disconcerted that he called his estranged parents, holding out an olive branch, asking them to come and rescue him. Sterling met them but was still in the dark. It was Sesnick who told him Lou had quit. And Sesnick who chose *Loaded*'s running order.

Lou of course resented the influx of fair-to-good reviews the band had been denied previously. Worse, it was Sesnick who retained the rights to the band name, despite Lou's best efforts. There were further subplots to all the resentment, with Sterling bemoaning Lou getting all the writing credits. "So now he's credited for being the absolute and singular genius of the Underground, which is not true. There are a lot of songs I should have co-authorship on, and the same holds true for John . . . but [Lou] wanted all the credit, more than we did, and he got it, to keep the peace."

Piece by piece, most of the original Velvets core had dispersed—Andy, Nico, John, now Lou. Yet like a movie villain who won't die, the name stayed afloat for now. Sterling, Moe, and Yule, with a Boston-born former bandmate of Yule's, Walter Powers, joining on bass, toured the States for much of 1971, Yule taking lead vocals and guitar. (The story goes that David Bowie excitedly came backstage to meet the Velvets, chatted effusively away about his fandom to the guy he thought was Lou Reed for ages, only to later be told he'd been talking to Doug Yule.)

In August, Sterling gave it up, after obtaining his degree from City College. He opted to study a PhD in medieval literature at the University of Texas in Austin. The final founder was gone. Willie Alexander, a singer-keyboardist and another friend of Doug's, was brought in. This short-lived lineup—dismissed by Danny Fields as "the Velveteen Underground"—played a few US and Canada shows in September and then did an October–November tour of the UK and the Netherlands, promoting *Loaded*. They disbanded in January '72.

When the release of *Live at Max's Kansas City* in May revived interest in Europe, Sesnick scored a one-album Polydor deal in the

UK. At his urging, Yule agreed to play a few British dates under the band name with guitarist Rob Norris, bassist George Kay, and drummer Mark Nauseef. But Sesnick didn't turn up in London and they were forced to play the gigs to get enough money to fly home. Even Yule had had enough by now, and called time in December.

Ever functional, he'd recorded that Polydor album while in London, with a couple of session musicians and Deep Purple drummer Ian Paice. (He'd wanted Tucker, but Sesnick said she was "too expensive." She, too, was now out.) On one level, *Squeeze*, released in February 1973, is the final Velvet Underground album. On another, as the rock critic fraternity has consistently grumped, it's that in name only. It's essentially a Doug Yule solo album. Even he was embarrassed when Sesnick ignored his extensive notes on how it should be mixed. "I gave what I had at the time," he said on a Doug Yule fansite. "There are parts of it I hate and parts of it I don't. If I had to do it again, it would be a completely different album, with different people. And have nothing to do with Sesnick." Reviews were inevitably rotten, Yule later deduced Sesnick had used it as a cash-grab, and Yule's "payment" from him was a paltry six copies of the album. Although it was an easy, lazy target for "worst albums of all time" lists for a couple of decades, in recent years it's been rather more kindly assessed. Chris Difford of the band Squeeze, who took their name from it, has said, "I really enjoy it. It has a kind of naivety about it." And indeed its light pop songs, plainly influenced by one particular aspect of Reed's writing, are at worst pleasant, at best curiously affecting.

But "pleasant" was never the benchmark for The Velvet Underground. When Doug and his brother, Billy, played a couple of gigs with George Kay and Don Silverman in Boston and Long Island, they were furious at finding themselves still billed under that name, and protested. Now it really was all over. Well, at least until the 1990s . . .

LIVE AT MAX'S KANSAS CITY

RECORDED
August 23, 1970, Max's Kansas
City, New York, NY

RELEASED
May 30, 1972

LABEL
Cotillion

PRODUCER
The Velvet Underground

PERSONNEL
Sterling Morrison (lead guitar,
backing vocals); Lou Reed (vocals,
rhythm guitar); Doug Yule (bass
guitar, backing vocals, lead vocal
on "I'm Set Free," "Lonesome
Cowboy Bill," "Who Loves the Sun,"
"I'll Be Your Mirror," "Candy Says,"
and "New Age"); Billy Yule (drums,
cowbell)

TRACK LIST
All songs written by Lou Reed,
except where noted

SIDE ONE
I'm Waiting for the Man
Sweet Jane
Lonesome Cowboy Bill
Beginning to See the Light

SIDE TWO
I'll Be Your Mirror
Pale Blue Eyes
Sunday Morning
   (Reed, John Cale)
New Age
Femme Fatale
After Hours

SQUEEZE

RECORDED
1972, London, UK

RELEASED
February 1973

LABEL
Polydor

PRODUCER
The Velvet Underground

PERSONNEL
Doug Yule (lead vocals, guitars, keyboards, bass guitar, producer); "Malcolm" (saxophone); Ian Paice (drums); unidentified female backing vocals

TRACK LIST
All songs written by Doug Yule

SIDE ONE
Little Jack
Crash
Caroline
Mean Old Man
Dopey Joe
Wordless

SIDE TWO
She'll Make You Cry
Friends
Send No Letter
Jack & Jane
Louise

Transformed: Lou Reed's solo career saw perfect days, kicks and sad songs.

9
CONEY ISLAND BABY

From "Make Up" to Metallica ... Lou Reed's Solo Sojourns

For all the charisma and talent of the various leading players in the Velvets' story, Lou Reed's tale magnetizes more than any other. Something about this often surly, belligerent, egocentric artist captivates us—his undoubted intelligence and raw creative instincts, sure, but also the sense that he was never just one thing, never predictable. His life and solo career after the Velvets painted this point time and again, always in colors which mutated both subtly and showily.

Transformer was takeoff. Solo and struggling after his half-hearted but better than people generally say it is debut album failed to launch, perma-shaded Lou, with a considerable platform-booted leg-up from flamboyant fanboy David Bowie, snatched a new career from the jaws of obscurity.

"I write about other people, tell stories, always did," Reed told me in 2004. "Any truly creative person could make five albums a year, easily. Each record is just what you did that week: another week, you might have done the same songs differently. But listen—I love every last one of them. Every single second of every last one, OK?"

OK. Fortunately for him and for us, in late 1972 what he did that week—to adapt an axiom of his—beat most people's year. *Transformer* remains a remarkable arranged marriage of gritty, witty words and pop succour. It anointed him the godfather of anti-stars, opening up a career which may otherwise have swiftly gone the way of all flesh.

"I don't have a personality of my own," said Reed in 1972. "I just pick up on other people's." He'd come to London for a change of pace, to "get out of the New York thing," but that first, eponymous, post-Velvets solo album, recorded on the dirty boulevards of Willesden Green (at Morgan Studios), had stuttered rather than strutted. Nobody, least of all him—pitched in record company ads as The Phantom of Rock—was quite sure where a former Velvet Underground front man should go next. This is where his personality came in, and plenty came out. Just five months after that debut, the November release of *Transformer* made him a household name in all the most disreputable households.

The world's fastest rising rock star, David Bowie, and his gifted lieutenant Mick Ronson, bang in the throes of Ziggy Stardust success, colored in Reed's persona. They coaxed forth the nervy, needy spirit of Warhol which Reed had ingested and brought him alabaster-faced into the glam rock era. They gave his unorthodox songwriting and unique vocal stylings the chance to step out of the gutter and into the spotlight. The cult of Lou became a small religion, as a freak hit single boosted his ego and confidence: a mixed blessing, given his reaction in the following years. *Transformer* remains a caustic, camp classic of palatable pop transgression.

Things moved quickly. As a devotee, Bowie had been namechecking the Velvets at every opportunity, playing their songs in his set for two years and even singing "Andy Warhol" on *Hunky Dory*. Perhaps calculating that he'd gain as much reflected cool as he'd give out, he whisked his American heroes and new pals—Reed and Iggy Pop—around London, showing them off to the press with much razzle-dazzle. Bowie saw in Iggy the wild, feral creature he was too cerebral to be; Reed, bookish too, arguably combined the essences of both. Yet Lou, for all his protestations about how pugnaciously perverse he was, was malleable. He wanted a career. He knew the "business people" were urging him to record with Bowie as the results would prove both vibrant and commercially viable. "And it turned out to be true, didn't it?" he smirked. Having always worn head-to-toe black, accustomed as he was to having films projected onto him, he allowed Angie Bowie to dress him more exotically. Going heavy on the black eyeliner, he briefly embraced being the Phantom of Rock. "I realised I could be anything I wanted," he drawled.

On July 8, he'd made his London debut, Bowie/Ziggy's guest at a Save the Whales benefit at the Royal Festival Hall. A week later, his solo gig sold out the Kings Cross Cinema, and he smiled as it sank in that the audience knew the words to his Velvets numbers. That's where Mick Rock shot the (fortuitously overexposed) live photo which became the album cover. On the back was a shot by Karl Stoecker, who'd already sealed his place in the higher echelons of rock imagery by photographing the first three Roxy Music album covers. It showed Reed's roadie/friend Ernie Thormahlen with a plastic banana erection and the model Gala (they were not the same person, though for years that rumor ran, tapping into the "he was a she" mythology). Years on, Reed sniffed, "I did three or four shows like that, then went back to leather. I was just kidding around. I'm not into makeup."

His new glam guru was. Bowie ushered him into Trident Studios in August. Sessions were rushed, as Bowie's other commitments, with Ziggymania breaking big, were escalating. Reed was on occasion of course grumpy. The glow of mutual adoration was fading. Yet gifted chief arranger Ronson and unflappable engineer Ken Scott (who'd produced *Ziggy*) caught lightning in a bottle.

Bowie had encouraged Reed to reveal tales and mysteries from his Factory years, to talk about the characters, the bathos and drama. He was eager to hear about underground New York—an impossibly glamorous notion to early seventies Brits. The album became a seedy but redemptive self-contained world, where the drive for love led individuals down wrong turns into impersonal sex and imperfect drugs. There was no better microcosm of this than in one of the most unexpected hit singles of its era. "Any song," wrote Nick Kent in the *NME*, "that mentions oral sex, male prostitution, methedrine and valium, and still gets Radio One airplay, must be truly cool."

"Walk on the Wild Side" is, along with "Perfect Day," the song for which the world at large will remember Reed, even if he fluctuated in later years between being grateful and deeming it a pain in the albatross. At the time of recording it was just another song, to his ears. His own preference for a single was the wiry rocker "Hangin' Round" "Which is why no-one listens to me."

As he'd recount during the 1978 shows at New York's Bottom Line (documented on the *Take No Prisoners* live album), he'd been approached by theatrical entrepreneurs in '71. They'd proposed the idea of adapting the 1956 Nelson Algren novel about vice and addiction, *A Walk on the Wild Side*. "Are you kidding?" protested Reed, true to his contrary nature. "It's about cripples in the ghetto. I'm the best qualified person to set music to a book about cripples in the ghetto??" He demurred, officially, yet—secretly flattered, perhaps—borrowed the title and sketched out ideas. Nudged first by Warhol, then by Bowie, he redrafted, peopling this backdrop with the Manhattan personalities he'd been transfixed by and "picked up on" around the Factory: Candy Darling, Joe Dallesandro ("Little Joe"), and Joseph Campbell ("the Sugar Plum Fairy") were members of Warhol's pansexual "Superstar" parade. This coterie of actors, artists, transvestites, junkies, and wannabes was both eulogized and mildly mocked by the song's taunting, partly ironic title. "If I retire now," Reed, having evidently warmed to it, said soon after its success, "'Walk on the Wild Side' is the one I'd want to be known by, my masterpiece. I found the secret with that song. That's the one that'll make them forget 'Heroin.'"

In fact, most of his new teenage audience in Britain, buying it because Bowie endorsed it, had never heard of "Heroin," and at that time barely registered the Velvets. *Transformer* served as a gateway drug. With radio DJs too naïve or dense to notice the sex and drugs references, the single climbed to No. 10 in the UK—albeit six months later—and broke in America. Herbie Flowers's two-note bass slide, baritone sax from Ronnie Ross (Bowie's sax teacher), and the "colored girls" going "doo da doo" allowed Reed's narration to drip with presence. He would pick the bones of New York for lyrical ideas ever more throughout a career of glorious highs and intriguing not-so-highs—not least on 1989's universally acclaimed "return to form," *New York*—but this inked his identity.

Still in thrall to the bohemian preachings of mentor-guru-poet Delmore Schwartz, he would fret about "selling out." Yet, as his tones oozed and seeped from radios around the world, the rare blend of sarcasm and soul had the knock-on effect of boosting the profile of Warhol's loosely related film trilogy of *Flesh*, *Heat*, and *Trash*. A debt repaid.

Warhol had also helped the genesis of "Vicious," the album's firm yet feathery opener. He'd suggested the title, adding, "You know, vicious like: I hit you with a flower." Ronson eases the riff along but goes for a flailing "Moonage Daydream"-style wig-out over the fade. To Lester Bangs, Reed declared it "a hate song," adding, "I drink constantly." On an otherwise deftly produced album, "Vicious" is oddly tame and muddy, but we do get the first dose of the pop-operatic backing vocals from Bowie which became such a key feature of *Transformer*.

The nursery rhymes from Purgatory continue with "Andy's Chest"—which Reed said was about Warhol's shooting by Valerie Solanas, "even though the lyrics don't sound like it." He'd first drafted it with the Velvets in 1969, but the Brits pulled back the tempo and highlighted the macabre imagery—bats, rattlesnakes, bloodsuckers. The new verse about Daisy May's belly button becoming her mouth was one step above music hall—"How'd she smell?" "Terrible!"—and Reed confessed he didn't know what it meant. "Swoop, swoop! Rock, rock!" went those delicious multitracked backing vocals, as Bowie and Scott enacted their current obsession with a kind of postmodern doo-wop.

It's easy to forget now that "Perfect Day" was "just" the hit's B-side (or technically a double A-side). Its surreal nineties crossover success as a family-favorite BBC charity commercial featuring Boyzone and Pavarotti meant that "25 years on, it became even bigger than Wild Side ever was," chuckled Reed. "Go figure." Back in 1972, it was already confusing and confounding people. Was this a beautiful sincere love ballad or a subversive hymn to smack? If the former, its tenderness—drink sangria in the park, feed animals in the zoo—felt authentic, topped by the Supremes-referencing "you keep me hanging on." Others insisted it was a dedication to Bettye Kronstad, who Reed—for all this album's overt sexual ambiguity—married in '73. Either way, Ronson's strings and piano capture the grandeur and frailty of falling in love. German artist (he designed the cover of *Revolver*) and Beatles ex-roommate Klaus Voormann played bass on the track (as he did on Carly Simon's "You're So Vain"). Even Reed was full of wonder for the musicians. Cast against type here, he was someone else, someone good.

"I'm really very inconsistent," muttered Reed. He's on more familiar ground in "Hangin' Round," its prickly put-downs laid down not long after Bowie and Ronson had bashed out Chuck Berry's "Round and Round." "Make Up" is fairly difficult to misinterpret: "We're coming out, out of our closets" was a slogan the Gay Liberation movement had adopted as a global rallying call. This tough guy's paean to lip gloss and perfume is enhanced by Herbie Flowers's tuba obbligato. "Wagon Wheel" and "I'm So Free" are conventional guitar chuggers which coast happily on the goodwill generated by the album around them: You can sense Ronson and Bowie trying a few minor twists here and there to jazz them up. "Satellite of Love," however, is another message from the gods.

The piano-driven arrangement, with finger-clicks and *those* backing vocals, echoes "Drive-In Saturday." Bowie soars stratospherically over the coda. Ken Scott has revealed that they could have made this climax even huger with what Bowie sang on mic, but the star insisted that this album had better be about Lou, not him. Reed displayed another rare flash of graciousness by acknowledging the majesty of this section. "It's not the kind of part I could ever have come up with, even if you'd left me alone with a computer program for a year. But David hears those parts, plus he's got a freaky voice and can go that high. It's very, very beautiful." The song in itself is no slouch, its sweetness turning sour through jealousy and paranoia. It had been demoed by the Velvets, but nothing like this. The narrator's comatose wonderment at technology—"I like to watch things on TV"—seemed to hint at Warhol's I-am-a-machine passivity then, but seems spookily prescient now. Addiction in another form.

"New York Telephone Conversation" is a gossipy send-up of Warhol's diaries, while the old-time jazz of "Goodnight Ladies"—led by Herbie and his tuba again—is the antithesis, except for the cynicism, of the Velvets. Reed was imagining his interior life as a nocturnal, nightmarish cabaret. Indeed on his next masterpiece, *Berlin*, he dropped these producers' pert pop arrangements and their style of dressing up his vignettes of sickly city life, and gambled on what Bob Ezrin called "a film for the ears." Perhaps he resented the kudos afforded his collaborators here. "He's very clever," he snarled of Bowie. "He learned how to be hip. Associating his name with me brought his name to a lot more people." Mercurial as ever, he later asserted, "I love him. He's very good in the studio. The kid's got everything. Everything."

Lou Reed changed his mind about *Transformer*, the album which made him a big noise and rebooted the arc of his autobiography, more times than he changed shirts. On its 25th anniversary reissue in 1997, he commissioned this writer to pen the liner notes, only to nix them because in a fit of revisionism he didn't want any mention, however passing, of "sexual experimentation." Seven years later than that, he told me he was thinking of remixing it. "That oughtta be fun. We could put Bowie's saxophone right at the back. We could mess around a whole lot." Such mischief. Today, it's safe to say most of us haven't changed *our* minds: It's a louche, landmark album which changed—transformed, as in increased the voltage of—his and countless lives.

His was after this a solo career of caustic cacophony and surprisingly sweet tenderness, never less than compulsively interesting, often magnificently muse-muzzling. Lou Reed famously changed that hyperactive mind of his frequently, regarding which of his songs he liked and which he loathed. His body of work after the dissolution of The Velvet Underground grew from uncertain beginnings through a prolific and wildly diverse seventies surge and on to a late eighties revival of inspiration. There were many turkeys along the way, as well as many triumphs. Every Lou Reed fan will, pretty much, have a different favorite among his albums.

Let's take a speedy, subjective "top twenty tracks" trip through its highlights. (These choices, opinions, and some omissions, will provoke some to wrath, but at least that's in the spirit of Lou (and the Velvets), plus we're "starting a conversation.") We can't squeeze everything into this operation, so while each have their advocates there's nothing in this specific roundup from those divisive fire-starters *Metal Machine Music* and *Lulu*. There's no "The Original Wrapper." Mercurial, contradictory, vaulting from throwaway garage-candy to high art concepts and back again, Lou Reed's enthralling, provocative solo catalog remains, years after his death (on October 27, 2013) aged seventy-one, as fascinating, frustrating, and full-on as the man himself.

* * *

Top 20 Lou Reed Tracks

㉠ "Magic and Loss (Summation)" (from _Magic and Loss_, 1992)

Lou's _Magic and Loss_ album, which he himself compared to Beethoven's Fifth, was a set of buttoned-up ponderings on cancer and death which came dressed as Lofty Art: Audiences who came to see him play it were barred from drinking or talking. Some believed his hype: Weirdly it's his highest-charting UK album (reaching No. 6). But it was no _Berlin_, bar this persuasive slow-burn finale about passing through fire.

㉑ "Tell It to Your Heart" (_Mistrial_, 1986)

"When I was thirty my attitude was bad." Yes, and your records were good. _Mistrial_ is, apart from the hilarious "The Original Wrapper," the sound of a forty-something man yelling at the telly from the sofa ("Video Violence"), and even Reed later bemoaned the production. Yet this closing curveball, where Lou mistakes a film set for a UFO, carried a sly hint of the ghost of _Transformer_.

㉘ "Set the Twilight Reeling" (_Set the Twilight Reeling_, 1996)

After a run of earnest, worthy, hark-at-me I'm-so-profound albums, it was a relief and release to hear him crank up the guitars again, even if it meant his interviews became yawnsome drones about amplifiers and studio technology. It's full of clumsy poetry, but this attempt to echo Dylan Thomas's "Do not go gentle . . ." does climax with a flare of the old heat.

17 "The Gun" (*The Blue Mask*, 1982)

The Blue Mask marked a new chapter, with a new, often loud guitar band. But its best moments involve restrained musical subtlety. Standout track "The Gun" has that, but also has Reed's sinister, deadpan narration covering violence, intimidation, home invasion, possibly rape. It's genuinely scary, reminding us that Reed had the genius to make a connection of music and words haunt your psyche.

16 "Vicious" (*Transformer*, 1972)

Transformer's tinselly tales made Lou a strange kind of pop star, and its opening simple-but-great guitar riff set free his new persona. With lines inspired by Warhol ("hit me with a flower") and Mick Ronson restraining himself until the fade, it's a great "hate song" despite the tinny production leaking much of its power.

15 "How Do You Speak to an Angel" (*Growing Up in Public*, 1980)

On the witty, intricately arranged *Growing Up in Public*, Reed takes one last long hard look at his various personalities before hitting forty. "I'm so damned sane," he said. This pomp-rock opener, all piano pirouettes and dovetailed dynamics, *a capella* blurts and handclaps, borders on Queen. Lou gives it conviction, asking how he's supposed to talk to pretty girls when his father was "weak" and "simpering."

14 **"Romeo Had Juliette"** (*New York*, **1989**)

Warhol died, Nico died, but Reed somehow pulled himself out of the eighties creative doldrums to deliver his most acclaimed album in many years, *New York*: so good he named it once. Its "fierce poetic journalism" (*Rolling Stone*) now called out, instead of wallowing in, urban squalor. Here, he chronicles the decaying ideals of his beloved city as it sinks and burns like the fall of Rome.

13 **"Kicks"** (*Coney Island Baby*, **1976**)

It's emblematic of Reed's career that as many fans think *Coney Island Baby* is a flaccid filler as rate it as one of his strongest. Following the willfully ugly *Metal Machine Music* with a tender, vulnerable pastiche of soul and doo-wop had everyone confused. Yet its mellow mood is broken by the incongruous, visceral fusion of words, music, muttering voices, and jolting sounds which constitute "Kicks." It's as if Reed's dark side is banging on the closet door, demanding to be let out. Sex, blood, and adrenaline: It's intense. (The bonus tracks on a reissue of the album feature Doug Yule on bass.)

12 **"Ennui"** (*Sally Can't Dance*, **1974**)

Reed claimed to hate *Sally Can't Dance* (his only US Top Ten album), but it's rich with wry asides. "Ennui," all but hidden away, is one of his frequent accidental not-trying-too-hard flashes of genius. It floats on a sullen mood, his voice so low it rumbles as he, cynical but arch, advises, "Pick up the pieces of your life / maybe someday you'll have a wife." Then he adds, "And alimony." That punch line's so unexpected that you laugh as you reel. "It's the track most people skip, I guess," said Lou. "It must be; it's the one I like."

⓫ "Disco Mystic" (*The Bells*, 1979)

"If you can't play rock and you can't play jazz," declared Lou, "put the two together and you've really got something." *The Bells* is a bizarre, bipolar mix of experiments in binaural sound and so-dumb-it's-smart pop, as if he'd noticed Bowie's Berlin wall-demolishing and fancied some of that. Hated by punk purists at the time, "proof" to them that Reed had "lost it," "Disco Mystic" is white funk if you ran it through a photocopier fifty times then drained its blood then got an Inauthenticity expert to triple-check it was fully inauthentic. Pastiche? Homage? It's stupidly, brilliantly funky. Either the least typical Lou Reed track of all time or, in its smirking ambivalent impishness, the most.

⓰ "How Do You Think It Feels" (*Berlin*, 1973)

Before side two of *Berlin* gets really dark, side one is merely very dark indeed. This straddles the line between autobiography and fiction ("speeding and lonely"), with Reed's phrasing urgent yet studied, and Alice Cooper's guitarists fully letting rip only once the story's told. A tangible plea for a reprieve from the horrors of existence and making love by proxy. The album's most upbeat track, then.

❾ "She's My Best Friend" (*Coney Island Baby*, 1976)

You could argue the case for "A Gift," which sighs, "I'm just a gift to the women of this world," as being one of *Coney Island*

Baby's highlights—"it's so funny," said Lou—but this old Velvets rough draft from 1968 is updated with terrific feel. The album's producer Godfrey Diamond never got due credit. An exquisite surge of rhythm and lead guitars mesh with Bowie-influenced call-and-response "la la la"s, and Reed gauges his vocal to build from confident to pleading. Either his most sincere or his most artificial love song.

8 **"Street Hassle" (*Street Hassle*, 1978)**
Part seedy punk, part cello-led rock opera, *Street Hassle* was, hoped Reed, a cross between "Burroughs, Selby, Chandler, Dostoevsky and rock 'n' roll. Dirty mainstream snot." The eleven-minute, three-movement title track sees those looped cellos circling like vultures as Lou tells a graphic (even by his standards) tale of ODs, "little girls," and "bad shit." And ultimately, ominously, inevitably, "bad luck." Probably the eeriest thing Bruce Springsteen has ever anonymously guested on.

7 **"Temporary Thing" (*Rock and Roll Heart*, 1976)**
Rock and Roll Heart, with Reed producing and playing all the guitars, was a confused response to CBGB punk, which he'd taken a while to grasp. "I'm too literate to be into punk rock," he'd snapped. It leaps between fiery riffs and self-parodying neo-jazz. Just when you're boxing it off, he pulls out this moody, willfully repetitive showstopper, a love-hate song, possibly about drugs, which feels clammy and grubby—you can smell it in your hair the next day. It's trashy, it's melodramatic, it's Reed *in excelsis*.

❻ "Walk on the Wild Side" (*Transformer*, 1972)

Yes, of course, this should be number one . . . but we're non-mainstream, hardcore obsessive fans here, right? (And if you're not being perverse and contrary, you're not doing Lou Reed right.) Whether Lou liked it or not (and he argued both sides depending on that day's mood swings), it's the song which made his post-Velvets name and by which the world at large remembers him. He didn't even think it was a single. Inspired by Nelson Algren and the colorful characters and pansexual "superstars" he'd met at the Factory, its atmosphere, created by Herbie Flowers's two-note bass slide, the backing vocals by Thunderthighs, and that baritone sax from Ronnie Ross, is immortal. Its purring sarcasm transformed his career.

❺ "The Bells" (*The Bells*, 1979)

Yep, we're *that* hardcore obsessive. Recorded in Germany, the left-handed jazz-rock of *The Bells* climaxes with this noir nine-minute electronic drone, punctuated with Don Cherry's wailing tributes to Ornette Coleman and semi-audible whispers and prayers. At the last, Reed's chipped voice breaks in, spontaneously reciting the story of a Broadway actor falling in ecstasy from a rooftop to his death. "The whole thing is a mood piece, supposed to cause an emotion," he explained. It does. Not an easy listen, it's inexplicably profoundly affecting.

❹ "Satellite of Love" (*Transformer*, 1972)

It had been demoed by the Velvets in the *Loaded* era, but not with this level of grace and grandeur. The Bowie-Ronson arrangement has the piano flourishing in all the right places and the backing vocals, finger clicks, and handclaps extracting the pop from the pomp. The lyric's main thrust seems to express a comatose wonderment at technology, with Reed as the missing link between Warhol's screen-entranced passive persona and Bowie as Thomas Jerome Newton.

❸ "Perfect Day" (*Transformer*, 1972)

It's frequently tricky to deduce whether Lou's being open-hearted or slyly sneering. Is "Perfect Day" a transcendent, vulnerable love song or a subversive paean to heroin? Of course, it's been taken out of his hands since, not least, insanely, by the likes of Boyzone and Pavarotti on the BBC's chart-topping 1997 Children in Need interpretation. Yet even upon *Transformer*'s release, most listeners heard genuine romance: sangria in the park, feeding animals in the zoo, and catching a movie worked as sincerity incarnate. We thought we were someone else. Someone good.

❷ "Sad Song" (*Berlin*, 1973)

Berlin, the most gothic thing ever made in Willesden, works best as a whole, especially the slide into unrelenting sorrow of its second half. Yet the great concept albums—"a film for the ears," producer Bob Ezrin called this—demand a big pay-off finish, and boy does *Berlin* bring that home. "Sad Song" is bombastic, but Reed's forlorn, muted voice contrasts perfectly with the *Sturm und Drang*. Every time you think his character's getting soft ("she looked like Mary, Queen of Scots"), he snaps back brutally ("just goes to show how wrong you can be"). They don't do mean-spirited melodrama like this anymore.

❶ "Coney Island Baby" (*Coney Island Baby*, 1976)

His pièce de résistance: A loping soul groove, deft doo-wop, and Bob Kulick's glistening guitar interjections knit a backdrop over which wannabe tough guy Reed drops the façade and exposes his youthful dreams and emotions ("I wanted to play football for the coach"). It's also a love letter to his transsexual muse, Rachel, who's explicitly namechecked. From the opening monologue's intimacy through the nod to The Five Keys' "The Glory of Love" (one of his favorite oldies), to the redemptive public-declaration-of-commitment punch line, "Coney Island Baby" is as sensitive as it is audacious, and, sonically, a glory. Reed's world was often "a funny place, something like a circus or a sewer," but here his better angels come shining through.

* * *

We mentioned there the gothic elements of, in particular, *Berlin*, and it's worth a brief tangent to ask if The Velvet Underground's enduring tagging as the pioneers of "goth" is valid, or merited. It also gives us a chance to probe *Berlin*, probably the greatest of all his albums.

Sure, notorious contrarian Lou may have said, "It wasn't the 'nocturnal' side of rock and roll—it was the daylight side. No one else had noticed it, that's all. We didn't know why everyone was reeling in shock." But the Velvets had an aura, and a taste in subject matter, as dark and shadowy as Edgar Allan Poe writing a story while watching *Suspiria* or *Bride of Frankenstein* in St. Vitus Cathedral. So were they gothic?

Firstly, gothic doesn't just mean goth. Yes, it conjures up images of spooky, morbid preoccupations and what Byron, discussing the work of Mary Shelley, once described as "pretty chills." We shiver in a kind of ecstasy at the best gothic films, books, and art. Yet the music movement labeled goth from around the early 1980s reveled too in a degree of glamour and camp, a sexy fatalism. Its roots came from various scraps of land, and there's an argument to be made that the Velvets watered the seeds as much as any forefather of the genre.

To go way back, working-class classical composer Havergal Brian (1876–1972), from Stoke-on-Trent, wrote a symphony called *The Gothic*, one of the longest symphonies ever composed. You'll find a larger number of claims made for Black Sabbath as the godfathers of goth. Ozzy Osbourne howled, "My name is Lucifer—please take my hand" on their 1970 debut album. Others might cite The Doors' "The End" (or perhaps Nico's version), or Leonard Cohen's wry couplets, or Iggy Pop's *The Idiot*, or Joy Division's drizzly gloom.

And as far back as the 1930s, bluesman Robert Johnson was singing of Faustian pacts and hellhounds on his trail. Gene Vincent raced with the devil. Folk music always reveled in murder ballads. Stravinsky and Carl Orff worked with the most ominous of sounds.

So it's hard to get a definitive agreement on when the bloodline of the gothic first mutated into goth music. What's certain is that it blossomed and proliferated in the eighties. The Cure, The Birthday Party, Siouxsie and the Banshees, The Damned, and others were active before the commonly perceived opening salvo—Bauhaus's "Bela Lugosi's Dead," released in August 1979. From then on, the willfully morose sighs of The Sisters of Mercy, The Mission, Cocteau Twins and company served as a counter to the multicolored, upbeat gaiety of most eighties pop (Wham!, Culture Club, Duran Duran et al.). The young and alienated, believing nobody understood them, and emphasizing that they never *asked* to be born, donned black and wallowed contentedly in goth music's message. Which was that it's all futile. Death, not love, conquers all.

From Batcave to bags of flour at Fields of the Nephilim gigs, it persisted. And endured in later decades through the likes of Marilyn Manson and Nine Inch Nails, and a loose rebranding as "emo." Goth was never without a leavening sense of humor though. Robert Smith of The Cure once told me, "I stare into mirrors and I hypnotize myself to see the devil in my face and skull." He wasn't being entirely serious.

So were these children of the night the spawn of the spirit of the Velvets? Of course, Lou Reed snapped (in 1977) that "I don't think I'm responsible for anything." That the Velvets were influential in many areas is undeniable. But in this field? I reckon so. They probed the heart of darkness/illumination, with both their sounds and their literacy, with a degree of fearlessness at which, say, the Beatles or Stones balked. Their sleazy, kinky mythology, annexed to Warhol's, was not for the fainthearted. Or rather, it offered the fainthearted a by-proxy, vicarious gateway to living by night.

Their opposition to slickness, their scoffing at conventional ideas of beauty, also mark them as goth's ancestors. And then there's Nico: surely a symbol of goth incarnate. The ever-enigmatic blonde (later anti-blonde) had her Fellini-related youth as just the beginnings of her boundless mystique: She didn't even have to wear shades like the others, unless she felt like it, to give off icy cool. Mixed into the milieu of Reed's word-pictures—"Heroin," "Venus in Furs," "All Tomorrow's Parties," and "Waiting for the Man" (this last later covered by Bauhaus)—her aloofness bolstered the barrage of sneers and shudders. That Velvets debut album doesn't *try* to be gothic, but it's brimful of the happily grotesque and enjoyable nefarious. *White Light/White Heat* was possibly even darker—"we stood for everything kids loved and parents hated" (Reed)—and you can find shock-horror thrills and spills in almost any line. "Lady Godiva's Operation," "The Gift," and "The Murder Mystery," like Lou's subsequent solo career, practically swam in gothic themes, as did Nico's and most certainly John Cale's.

After "Walk on the Wild Side" gave him that unlikely hit, Reed reacted by overcompensating—how very like him—and recording "difficult" albums which demanded much of his fragmenting fan base. This went on all his life. They danced with degrees of darkness from the perverse *Metal Machine Music* (if that isn't scary, what is?) to the deep-noir narratives of *Street Hassle* or *The Bells*; from the investigations of mortality running through *Songs for Drella* (with Cale) and *Magic and Loss* to the Poe-inspired *Raven*, one of the most consciously gothic records ever made.

Surely his masterpiece of the mood is, however, 1973's *Berlin*. It drew alarming bile and vitriol from critics, so it must've been doing something right. They'd expected a sensible commercial career move. They got, as producer Bob Ezrin put it, "a film for the ears." Ezrin himself was young, ambitious, and fearless. High on his recent success with Alice Cooper (another character not averse to Gothic trappings and grand guignol), Ezrin would in later years go on to help build Pink Floyd's *The Wall*, Roger Waters's neo-gothic cry for help.

Constructing *Berlin*, both Reed and Ezrin pushed themselves to the verge of nervous breakdown. When it was completed, Ezrin suggested to Reed that "the best idea is we put it in a box, put the box in a closet, leave it there and never listen to it again." Totally uncompromising in its stark, bleak candor, it felt like a kind of exorcism of demons. The irony, perhaps, is that it's a beautiful work of art, and gorgeous (if unbearably moving) to listen to.

"We killed ourselves psychologically on that record," said Lou. "We went so far into it that it was hard to get out." Its story of a doomed, needy *ménage à trois* in the titular city (itself a potent symbol) covered obsessive jealousy, domestic violence, drugs (of course), comedowns, bad parenting, and suicide. The music was baroque, bruising/bruised rock opera, with Reed's ultra-dry, ennui-riddled monotone only emphasizing the angst and grandeur. "The narrator is filling you in from his point of view," he offered. "And his point of view is not particularly pleasant."

Some simplistically suggested Nico was the muse. Reed snapped, "She didn't understand a word of it." The album's reception broke Reed's heart, contributing to his lifelong prickliness toward journalists. The bombing of *Berlin* was the biggest disappointment of his career, he confessed. "I pulled the blinds down shut at that point . . . and they've remained closed." Nevertheless, he drove on with his murky, sunless subject matter. His last album, the equally cruelly reviewed *Lulu*, a collaboration with Metallica, delved into sexual abuse and Jack the Ripper. He told me, "It's not a party record. The mind is the most erogenous zone I know. This is where I like to exist." And anyone intrigued with the nocturnal notions of the gothic will empathize with that.

From Cohen to Cooper to The Cure, from Bauhaus to the Banshees to Billie Eilish, "goth"—or the gothic in music—is a shape-shifter, adapting its form to accommodate and express its small hopes and large sorrows. Its aim is to transcend. "We loved with a love that was more than love," wrote Edgar Allan Poe. The Velvets, and Lou Reed, always strived to subvert the norm and twist the structures, to find the dream within the dream. Stephen King, eulogizing H. P. Lovecraft, opined that the essence of the gothic was "the voice whispering from inside the pillow."

Reed, as a writer, always had access to that voice. The Velvet Underground was perhaps the first rock group to have it on speed dial.

* * *

Lou never really mellowed, at least not when growing up in public. When he made his final album in 2011 with Metallica, the Velvets' nineties reunion a faint memory by now, he was still proving he could be as unpredictable and provocative as ever. I was sent to interview the new best pals for *Classic Rock* in 2011. It wasn't a tea party. With a shudder and smile I remember it thus . . .

As I'm thrust into a suite at Claridge's in London with four cameramen for company plus a girl pointing a fluffy boom mic up my nose, the sight of Lou Reed, James Hetfield, and Lars Ulrich sitting on sofas opposite is oddly reassuring. Freaky, and faintly terrifying, obviously, but reassuring to the degree that the story that Lou Reed and Metallica have made an album together, based on a relatively obscure play much admired by Sigmund Freud, may not have been the deranged fantasy of an Internet rumor-monger on disagreeable steroids.

Like a restricted view of Mount Rushmore, or the protagonists of *Sons of Anarchy* after a lottery win and a good wash, the three rock gods stare at me, silent, impassive, possibly a bit knackered on this opening day of promo. Someone mutters, "Good to go." To ease us all in, I ask the obvious question; entirely non-confrontational. So, I say mildly to a safe midpoint between Lou (seated left) and James and Lars (seated right), how did this surprising collaboration come about?

"*Why*??" rumbles a gruff voice from deep within Lou Reed's bowels. He's a physically small man, frail, sixty-nine years old. He moves carefully. But when he glares at you, believe me, you *stay* glared at. "*Why* is it surprising?" barks that leathery, bespectacled, iconic face.

Uh ... two completely different genres ... merging ...

"And *that's* surprising?" he snaps. "*Who would say that?*"

We've been going twenty-five seconds. I'm not convinced it's going well. Then again, as mentioned earlier in this book, Reed once told me an interview had "started well, but now your questions suck," and in 2004, when I asked if he was clean-living these days, drawled, "Oh I'm smoking a fucking crack-pipe as we speak, can't you tell?" So, you know, maybe this counts as promising.

He demands to know which specific people on which specific websites have said this collaboration is "surprising." Instinctively, I start answering back, just random words really, realize I have no idea and that anyway this isn't the point, then turn around to the director filming the interviews and suggest we take this from the top. Lou, suddenly an impish, naughty little boy, goes, "But I only got to 'Why?' I was going to then move to where, when, in which language—English? Danish? In *Esperanto*?" There's a twinkle in his eyes (he's short-sighted) and he's working hard not to laugh. "Go on," he decrees. "Carry on, this'll be good." He all but winks. He's just messing about. (Half a century of picking fights with interviewers must be a hard habit to break. "I've hidden behind the myth of Lou Reed for years," he once said. "I can blame anything outrageous on him. I'm so easily seduced by the public image of Lou Reed that I'm in love with Lou Reed myself.") From here on, he's a pussycat, talking at length and with smarts, even out-talking Lars, which is unheard of.

During the bulk of the interview, the unlikely alpha trinity of Loutallica are at ease (if a little overtly—"after you, no, after you, I insist"), singing each other's praises, the air thick with mutual respect, all on message that *Lulu* is happening. Like it or not, believe it or not, it's well and truly happening. "My Lulu had a head," says Reed today, "but she needed a body."

"It's not a party record," he observes. "It's not one of those: 'Hey baby, you sucked my dick, now let's do a line of coke and get a tattoo on the weekend and make believe and see you later at grad school, hurrah.'"

He pauses. "OK," he muses. "So it's *not* that."

The venerable dark prince of New York avant-rock made unconscionably influential music with The Velvet Underground in the sixties before becoming a solo star on the back of Bowie collaboration *Transformer* and has since released a stream of diverse albums, from the punk tangent *Street Hassle* to the cacophonic *Metal Machine Music*, channeling the spirit of Burroughs and Poe. It's safe to say he thinks. Metallica, the world's best-selling thrash metal band (a hundred million albums sold) have been wrangling speed and volume to shape sound in new ways ("Ride the Lightning," "Master of Puppets") since forming in California in '81. It's safe to say they rock. Today, Reed mentions in passing Tennessee Williams, David Cronenberg, and the composer Strauss. James Hetfield says of the album, "We got to stamp *'Tallica* on it, y'know? To make it *heavy*." Lars says a lot of things, admittedly after turning to the others and politely saying to them, "Shall I do the spiel then?" "Yeah," says Lou, "you're so good at it." "Oh, thank you!"

beams Lars, "and that's coming from *you!*" I also talk to guitarist Kirk Hammett and bassist Rob Trujillo, who are equally enthusiastic. "On paper it does look strange," says Kirk. "No-one else in the heavy metal world has done anything like this. It's a new animal." "It'll definitely freak some people out," says Rob, "and that's good."

If you think about sex, death, and alienation, and you probably do, the album isn't so very unlikely. Both parties have consistently dealt with these subjects lyrically, just with contrasting skill sets. The clash-marriage-collision-bonding of the two has delivered something as startling and strange as you'd expect, only more so. It works (and works you hard) on visceral and cerebral levels. Its ninety minutes of noise and neuroses are inspired by the "Lulu" plays (*Earth Spirit* and *Pandora's Box*), written by German expressionist Frank Wedekind. These plays (originally penned in 1894 and 1904 respectively), hugely controversial then and scarcely less so now, flash between the points of view of Lulu (a seductress-victim-Eve-mirror) and her lovers and abusers. There's plenty of sex. Also, Jack the Ripper shows up, so there's violence. Director-choreographer Robert Wilson hired Reed to come up with lyrics and songs for his modern theatrical production in Berlin (a city close to Reed's creative heart since his macabre, brilliant 1973 album of that name). Overriding another mooted plan, Reed, in Ulrich's words, "asked if we were game. And we've been forever touched and changed by the experience." "We wanted to add to the potency," says Hetfield, "to make it ROCK." "This is the best thing I ever did," announces Reed, "and I did it with the best guys I could possibly find on this planet."

How, though, did these new best friends meet, plan to record, and then retain the focus, sometime later, to get together and do it? Lars does the spiel. They first came together in October 2009 at the 25th Anniversary of the Rock and Roll Hall of Fame concerts, Metallica playing "Sweet Jane" and "White Light/White Heat" onstage at Madison Square Garden with Lou, who declares, "We knew from then that we were made for each other." According to Lars, Metallica had been invited to host and represent "the left-field artists, the outsiders." Reed was "top of our list to collaborate with" because "he's like a solo version of Metallica, always done his own thing, reinvented himself, challenging not only himself but his fans." It felt "effortless." Lou then suggested that they record together. Metallica "ran around the world three times" finishing their *Death Magnetic* commitments, and were "ready." Lou's first idea was to record "some lost Lou Reed jewels," continues Lars, "and we'd do whatever it is we do to those songs." That strategy hung in the air awhile. A week or two before sessions were to begin, Lou called up and sold them his "Lulu" plan. The band were intrigued, Hetfield happy to "take off my singer and lyricist hat and concentrate on the music, to put our 'stamp' on it." "Stamp?" laughs Reed. "It's *branded*. And it's not coming out."

Kirk reveals that the band was much happier with this arrangement, it being a spontaneous collaboration rather than Metallica playing on already established songs. "We bowed to the magic." Lars talks of being "psyched" by the structureless nature of Reed's songs and of "inventing the wheel"; Hetfield of a "blank canvas." They've tried before, they say, but never been this "far out there." It was "authentic, impulsive . . . an exciting ride to be on."

If there is any area in which the happy gang don't quite have their story straight—and you have to squint to find it—it's the slight gap between Metallica labeling the material Reed brought along as a "blank canvas" and Reed's notion of them as songs. Put this down to everyone enthusiastically claiming credit: It's honest, boyish zeal all round rather than ego-niggling. That he gave them "atmospheres, sound-scapes" seems to be the consensus, and they fleshed them out. (And lengthily— most of the ten tracks are in the region of ten minutes: "Junior Dad" runs, with strings and drones, to nineteen.) Reed laughs heartily when I ask Metallica if the project took them out of their comfort zone. "Have you *heard* their comfort zone?" he says. He's not reluctant, however, to emphasize that the ball started rolling with him. After one speech, it dawns on him that he's hogging the interview, and he mutters good-naturedly at Lars and James, "I'll stop, I'll just stop . . ." "I'm enjoying everything you're saying!" says Lars, beaming. "Keep going! Ha ha!" Only the faintly awestruck "ha ha" hints at an excess of eagerness to please. "I'm enjoying it too, it's good stuff," I say, but in truth the three of them are performing for each other, demonstrating how into it they are, barely aware I'm still here. When later I'm signaled to wrap things up, Lars says, "Oh give yourself five more minutes man!" James murmurs dryly, "We're talking here. It's a wonder anything gets done!"

"I'd worked on this thing for a while," affirms Lou, possibly making sure nobody runs away with the notion that Metallica did all the heavy lifting. He gives a backstory of the "immoral, no, *amoral*" play: How shocking to the bourgeois it was in its day "which I guess is why Wedekind wrote it." He describes Lulu as the great "femme fatale," and I'm not the only one in the room who gets a buzz off hearing Reed use the words "femme fatale" in the course of a sentence. Lou got what he calls his "paws" on it, and spent time fathoming the narrative with "my significant other, Laurie Anderson." It didn't come easy. "We had to figure out Lulu's psychology, to bring her to life in a sophisticated way, but using rock." He wanted "the hardest power rock you could come up with," and "Metallica live on that planet." "Dream come true," he nods.

He sent Lars some roughs. James says, "We sat there with an acoustic guitar, listening, and just let it take us where it needed to go. It was a great gift, starting from scratch . . ." Lou stays silent but his presence abides and James switches horses midstream. "Well, there *was* a body of work there, very potent lyrics, and . . . we got it together very quickly." Lou turned up at Metallica's HQ studios in California on a Monday in April and, says Lars, "by lunchtime, we were fucking deep in it. Jamming, playing, throwing paint at the canvas. Happily and hopefully all the 'record' buttons in the cockpit were on." (Lou eulogizes HQ: "magnificent for real power and feeling and emotion.") Whereas Metallica are notorious for spending ages in preparation, agonizing over every riff, Lou's rigid stares would let them know that the extended improv they'd just let loose with was a "take." "It was intuitive," adds Lars, "I mean—thirty years here, but it was just so exciting to just . . . go. To just feel it, respond to what was going on." Work was finished in under a month.

"They said: let's go, let's do it, can't wait," says Lou. "I'd been submerging my psyche in Lulu and the various characters, and in the studio we'd examine this further. It's not always Lulu singing; in my mind I'm switching gears, characters. It's not easy. It's like: what happens if you try to bring the whole thing up to the level of Selby, Poe, Burroughs, Inge, Tennessee Williams? There's an argument that if you have to think, you can't rock. But the mind is the most erogenous zone I know, so that's an unusually dumb comment."

James enjoyed the fact that there was "another powerful force in the room." After a feeling-out period, "I'd think: I maybe don't like that part, but should I say something? I don't want to shut the door on stuff because I've been called 'Dr. No' for twenty years. But now I'm almost the opposite, I couldn't stop saying yes! We needed to agree that this was just *awesome*. Who's steering the ship at that point? The moment is. Let go of that fear of no control, and you're in Heaven. So many great ideas coming at once: don't mess with them. Celebrate that. A wonderful problem to have."

"Lou's very literate," says Kirk. "He doesn't take any shit," says Rob. Kirk adds that the band tuned their guitars down "to C" to give Lou more range vocally. "That helped him greatly." Asked if there were happy accidents, Lars says, "The whole thing was one happy accident after another." James says, "There's no accidents here. This was supposed to happen. I absolutely know that." "Oh me too," concurs Lou. "We happened to kinda meet by accident, but again, there's no such thing as an accident. I don't think we ever disagreed about anything. It was just five guys trying to do this thing, whatever it was."

Whatever it is, it's not, as Reed rightly points out, a party record. With its unblinking beat lyrics and rants of jealousy, lust, violence, and revenge, and its grinding riffs, tantalizing tones, and taxing drones, it's a turbulent, caustic, grueling, exhausting, uncompromising ninety-minute voyage into . . .

"I wouldn't call it the heart of darkness," muses Reed. "I'd call it the heart of illumination."

"It could be disturbing," suggests Rob. "At the same time, it could be beautiful. It's a marriage of attitudes. I personally feel that Lou's made us a better band, more creative, which will definitely help us in future. It's something special either way, at the end of all this." "It's next level," says Kirk. "I hope our fans embrace it with an open mind. We're kindred spirits, for sure. Mesh us together, it creates something graphic, cinematic *and* heavy."

"There they were," declares Lou. "Pushing me to the best I've ever been. By definition, everybody in there was honest. You say it's an 'odd' collaboration? An 'odd' collaboration would be Metallica and Cher. This is an obvious one." "Lou knows," says James, "I've been searching for something like this for a while. We needed it."

So, is it a one-off? Will this go down as one of rock's most historic head-to-heads/triumphs/debacles? Or are these loved-up best buds, these contrasts-in-arms, in for the duration? "We never go that far in our thinking," says Reed. "It's enough to me that we're even on this planet. This thing has been shepherded into the world unsullied and will go out the way it came in. Pure. This is a new genre here, and we punch it out. This is where I like to exist."

And that was the last time I met Lou Reed.

When we were done, he chatted amiably for ten more minutes about his recent solo shows. Beneath the bravado, he was delicate, like a bronze head atop a body made of rice paper. Rising slowly, very slowly, to leave, he shook my hand four times.

A few months previously, I'd seen him play at the Hammersmith Apollo. Notoriously, Reed's live shows could go either way. Over the decades, you might have caught him emitting an hour of white noise, noodling over one precious chord change, ranting for no clear reason, or applauding an onstage tai chi dancer. Tonight, our luck's in. Onstage is the man who fronted The Velvet Underground before unleashing a stream of diversely brilliant seventies solo albums and carving a willfully provocative career of peaks and troughs which has quested after a perverse, dirty purity. From minute one, he and his exquisite band (who he conducts, cajoles, and directs) are utterly spellbinding.

This type of show—quivering on the brink of collapse yet always swooping away to triumph—is what becomes a legend most.

Walking on, he seems frail, tentative, but once in character he appears indomitable. After a timid "Who Loves the Sun," a blistering "Senselessly Cruel" lets us know Lou, pushing seventy and moving like it, is up for it. His set-list seems designed for clued-up Reed fans rather than those wanting what we'll call, at a stretch, the "hits." "Temporary Thing" is a transcendent minimalist mantra of repressed rage. His brave take on John Lennon's "Mother" is startling, Reed's risky phrasing lurching between genius and ill-advised and therefore at its most heroic, while "Venus in Furs" purrs. Acoustic, stripped-down breezes through "Sunday Morning" and "Femme Fatale" allow us to assimilate what we just witnessed. After the inevitable "Sweet Jane," the encore is his rarely performed jazz trip "The Bells." It's epic. One for the ages, this.

"I love you Lou!" shouts one voice among the awed crowd. "After all this time," he deadpans, "you must know that I love you too."

I'm sticking with you: The Velvets (Tucker, Morrison, Reed, Cale) reunited at Black Island Studio, London, 1993.

10
THAT'S THE STORY OF MY LIFE: INTO THE AFTER HOURS

A fter hours, as time began to see the light, the Velvets mythology grew and grew. Reality was also complicating and confusing the narrative. Even before *Squeeze* was released, even before Reed's resurgence, Lou, John Cale, and Nico had set aside their differences to play a show as a trio in Paris, at Le Bataclan, in January 1972. Broadcast on French TV, much bootlegged since, it at last got an official release in 2004. Presented as *Le Bataclan '72* by Lou Reed, John Cale, and Nico, it proved—generally somber as it is—that all three were content to play the better-known Velvets songs, as well as individual moments. Because by now solo careers were very much ongoing, despite the Paris gig fueling hopes of a full reunion.

Reed, having taken time out in Long Island at his parents', and even taking a job as a typist at his father's accountancy firm, signed with RCA in '71, and undertook the solo career we've just examined. Nico had gone solo as early as 1967, with her *Chelsea Girl* album a significant spin-off to the Velvets saga. Released by Verve and produced by Tom Wilson, it featured writing and playing contributions from Reed, Cale, and Morrison. These included the Reed-Morrison track "Chelsea Girls," "Wrap Your Troubles in Dreams" (an early Velvets live number, their recorded version of which didn't emerge until the 1995 *Peel Slowly and See* box set), Cale's "Winter Song," Cale and Reed's "Little Sister," and "It Was a Pleasure Then," credited to Reed/

Cale/Nico. She also interpreted two Jackson Browne songs, of which "These Days" has survived as a landmark of Nico's unique melancholy. Her take on Bob Dylan's "I'll Keep It with Mine" and Tim Hardin's "Eulogy to Lenny Bruce" are also among her most striking, unsettling, work. True to pattern, she was unhappy with the album upon release, as the stripped-down chamber folk she'd envisaged had, without her consent, been dressed up with string and flute overdubs by Wilson and arranger Larry Fallon. "I still cannot listen to it," she said in '81 in the notes to a reissue of the Velvets' debut. "Everything I wanted for that record, they took away. The first time I heard the album I cried, and it was all because of the flute . . ." *Trouser Press* agreed it was "sabotaged by tepid arrangements." Yet others insist it's a masterpiece. Nobody disputes that the cover photography, by Paul Morrissey and Billy Name, is as iconic as that overused adjective gets. In an interview with Pat Patterson for *IN New York*, reprinted on the album's inner sleeve, Nico said, "I try to remain alone as much as I can . . . I like sad songs, tragic ones . . . I just can't be around anything that is forced, I'd rather just remain how I feel . . ."

For 1968's *The Marble Index*, she wrote her own songs, singing and playing harmonium (her signature sound from here on), freeing herself from the Velvets to a degree, although only a degree. John Cale brought arrangements and added folk and classical instruments. Urged by Jim Morrison of The Doors, who she called her soul brother, to write lyrics infused with poetry, she dyed her hair and wore black as she tried to put her model image behind her. "She hated the idea of being blonde and beautiful," said Cale to *Uncut* magazine. "*The Marble Index* was an opportunity for her to prove she was a serious artist." Its chilly, bleak soundscape has often been anointed as anticipating goth.

Others have designated it the ultimate heroin album. Its alienating yet magnetizing power slow-burned its way to considerable influence.

Cale produced and played on her next two albums, 1970's *Desertshore* (of which Björk and Bat for Lashes are professed fans) and 1974's *The End* (featuring Brian Eno and Phil Manzanera of Roxy Music), her last album for seven years. In that same year she opened for Tangerine Dream at their epochal Reims Cathedral concert. Cale, meanwhile, was eternally adaptable, inventive, and productive.

As a producer alone he's carved his likeness into the Mount Rushmore of rock music. After the first two Nico albums in stark contrast, he produced The Stooges' debut album. Dismissed initially as stupid, tasteless, and childish (among other things), it's now—as "I Wanna Be Your Dog" and "No Fun" refuse to stop blazing—established as *the* primordial proto-punk classic. (Cale's mix was rejected by Elektra for the first release; the label president and Iggy Pop took over.) He then worked on Nick Drake's *Bryter Later*, and with Eno, before producing Patti Smith's classic *Horses* in '75, Smith having loved the raw sound of his solo album *Fear*. Smith later spoke of ego clashes—she'd needed a technical person but got "a total maniac artist," before concluding to *Rolling Stone*, "He had me so nuts I wound up doing this nine-minute cut that transcended anything I ever did before." Cale's subsequent production or collaboration catalog reads like a frenetic flight through the evolution/devolution of rock, from Jonathan Richman's Modern Lovers, Squeeze, and Sham 69 to Happy Mondays' 1987 debut album and Siouxsie and the Banshees' *The Rapture*. By 2010, he was guesting on a Manic Street Preachers album.

In the immediate wake of the Velvets' demise, however, he was impressing with the beginnings of his own enduring solo work.

Vintage Violence (1970) was curiously close in places to American soft rock, as if he was trying to suppress his own avant-garde instincts, but these came out on *Church of Anthrax* (with Terry Riley), and through the seventies on the likes of *Fear* (arguably his best), *Slow Dazzle* (featuring an extraordinary reinvention of "Heartbreak Hotel"), and *Helen of Troy*. He'd moved back to the UK in '73 and signed a productive six-album deal with Island. Throughout his oeuvre, his tender and aggressive sides arm-wrestle. His provocateur days were not forsaken: At a gig in Croydon in 1977 he decapitated a dead chicken with a meat cleaver.

He had drug addiction issues which he later confessed became "embarrassing," and cleaned up his act after the birth of his daughter Eden in '85. "You take drugs thinking, Wow, I'm going to get through a lot of work," he told Simon Price for *The Independent*. "And I guess I did, but nothing like what I got through without them . . . you don't have an idea of how time passes when you're in that state." It wasn't long before *Arena Homme Plus* was summing up New Reformed Cale as "iconoclast, polymath, performer, thinker, classical composer, rabble rouser, rock 'n' roll savage, professional musical schizophrenic, cyber punk and father." He was all these things when he readied himself to reconvene with Reed for 1990's catalyst for the Velvets reunion, *Songs for Drella*.

As Reed's reputation rose after the triumph of *Transformer*, and David Bowie was among those eulogizing the Velvets' records, Sterling Morrison and Moe Tucker were enjoying much quieter profiles. By the mid-seventies, Sterling was struggling as a Medieval Literature assistant professor in Texas, and he took work as a deckhand on Houston tugboats to make ends meet. He gained a license as a master

VU

RECORDED
1968–69, New York, NY

RELEASED
February 1985

LABEL
Verve

PRODUCER
The Velvet Underground

PERSONNEL
John Cale (viola, celesta and backing vocals on "Stephanie Says," bass guitar and backing vocals on "Temptation Inside Your Heart"); Sterling Morrison (guitar, backing vocals); Lou Reed (vocals, guitar); Maureen Tucker (drums and percussion, lead vocals on "I'm Sticking with You"); Doug Yule (bass guitar, keyboards, lead vocals on "She's My Best Friend," backing vocals on "I Can't Stand It," "Lisa Says," "Foggy Notion," "One of These Days," and "Andy's Chest," piano and backing vocals on "I'm Sticking with You," lead guitar on "One of These Days")

TRACK LIST
All songs written by Lou Reed, except where noted

SIDE ONE
Recorded May 20, 1969
  I Can't Stand It
Recorded February 13, 1968
  Stephanie Says
Recorded May 14, 1969
  She's My Best Friend
Recorded October 1, 1969
  Lisa Says
Recorded June 19, 1969
  Ocean

SIDE TWO
Recorded May 6, 1969
  Foggy Notion (Reed, Sterling Morrison, Doug Yule, Maureen Tucker, Hy Weiss)
Recorded February 14, 1968
  Temptation Inside Your Heart
Recorded September 23, 1969
  One of These Days
Recorded May 13, 1969
  Andy's Chest
  I'm Sticking with You

mariner and soon captained a tugboat, swimming with the flow of this through the eighties. He played in a few bands locally from time to time, purely for fun.

Tucker had upped sticks to Phoenix, Arizona, to raise a family with her husband (they divorced in the mid-eighties) and five children. Around the time of her divorce, the music bug struck again and she released several small-scale independent albums, singing and playing guitar. Sterling was a sometime member of her band. Her 1982 debut, *Playin' Possum*, where she plays every note, attempts everything from "Louie Louie" to a nine-minute take on "Heroin." She also worked in a Wal-Mart warehouse in Tucson as a computer operator. After she quit that job, Lou Reed and various members of Sonic Youth were among those guesting on 1989's busier, fuller *Life In Exile After Abdication*, which ran through "Pale Blue Eyes" and a Tucker composition named "Andy." Doug Yule, meanwhile, popped up playing guitar on sessions for the Reed albums *Sally Can't Dance* and *Coney Island Baby*.

The reverence in which the Velvets were held hollered even louder after the February 1985 release by Verve of the thrillingly revelatory *VU*, which at last gathered the unreleased tracks, now cleaned up, from that so-called "lost" album (several of which Reed had since reworked on his solo records). Ranked the third best album of that year by *NME*, it's lithe, loose, and spirited. The atypical "I'm Sticking with You," sung by Maureen, even showed up in a 2002 Hyundai ad, and on the soundtrack of Oscar-winning 2007 film *Juno*. We're a long way from Warhol screen tests. A year on, *Another View* repeated the trick, with "We're Gonna Have a Real Good Time Together," which Reed had since idiosyncratically recycled on *Street Hassle*, leading the charge.

Even Václav Havel, Czech playwright turned politician, hailed the band as inspiration when he became a protagonist in ending four decades of Communist rule in his country, in the "Velvet Revolution." He and Reed buddied up. The Velvets' stock was high; they were the coolest of names to drop. The UK's prestigious arts series *The South Bank Show* dedicated a 1986 special to them, wherein the members discussed forming and splitting, the contrast between the popular music of the era and their dissonant style, and the New York art scene of the sixties. Cale said the real reason they wore dark glasses onstage was because they couldn't stand the sight of their audiences. Critics pored over their significance and there were rare clips of the band as well as excerpts from Warhol films. Bowie and Johnny Rotten spoke. Mary Harron, later to direct the films *I Shot Andy Warhol* and *American Psycho*, was a researcher. The Velvets were, not to mince words, hip again. Rumors of a reunion swelled.

But before the magic, some loss.

Having sashayed through the very-different-to-the-Factory kind of glamour of Studio 54 in the seventies and swanned through the eighties as a celebrity "business artist"—"everything's plastic, but I love plastic ... I want to be plastic"—Andy Warhol was both resiliently credible (affiliating with younger artists like Jean-Michel Basquiat and Julian Schnabel) and still eagerly hanging out with the latest hot band on the block (from Blondie to Psychedelic Furs to Duran Duran). That said, he'd become relatively more reflective and cautious after radical feminist writer and *Scum* manifesto author Valerie Solanas shot him in 1968, seriously wounding him. In February 1987, he died, aged just fifty-eight, after gall bladder surgery at New York Hospital. He'd been ill for some time and delayed treatment, scared of hospitals. His family sued the hospital, receiving a large settlement. He was buried south of Pittsburgh next to his parents. He is arguably the most famous artist since Picasso.

The following year, Nico died, aged forty-nine. Living between Manchester and London, she'd managed a moderate though short of glorious career revival, touring as a doomy cult figure, and releasing an excellent final album, *Camera Obscura*, with Cale again producing, in 1985. (She also toured as Cale's support act in '87.) Her version of "My Funny Valentine" remains wonderfully poignant. When in 2010 Simon Price of *The Independent* asked if it had been tough seeing his friend and former lover in a state of decline, Cale sighed philosophically, "Everyone organizes their life the way they can. She organized hers around a drug. There was always this moment in the studio when there would be tears. She'd go away, you'd do your adorning of the tracks, you'd play back the finished product, then there would be tears of happiness: 'Ohhh, eet ees beautiful!'"

Her on-off heroin addiction is much documented, and she was rarely hailed as an easy personality to rub along with. In July '88, she took a holiday in Ibiza with her son, Ari, with whom she was rebuilding her relationship. She fell off her bicycle, suffering a cerebral hemorrhage. Although some have pointed out the irony of a junkie dying while on a healthy bike ride on a sunny day, her son said that she'd set off to buy marijuana. Nobody from the Velvets or the Factory world went to her funeral in Germany.

Her influence, her aura, did linger. In 2009 Cale put together a traveling tribute show, *Along the Borderline*, with various guest vocalists expressing their fandom. "The point was that there's a rich

ANOTHER VIEW

RECORDED
1967–69, New York, NY

RELEASED
September 1986

LABEL
Verve

PRODUCER
The Velvet Underground

PERSONNEL
John Cale (viola on "Hey Mr. Rain" (version I) and "Hey Mr. Rain" (version II), bass guitar on "Guess I'm Falling in Love"); Sterling Morrison (guitar, backing vocals, bass guitar on "Hey Mr. Rain"); Lou Reed (vocals, guitar, piano); Maureen Tucker (drums and percussion); Doug Yule (bass guitar, keyboards, backing vocals)

TRACK LIST
All songs written by Lou Reed, except where noted

SIDE ONE
Recorded September 30, 1969
   We're Gonna Have a Real Good Time Together
Recorded September 27, 1969
   I'm Gonna Move Right In (Reed, Doug Yule, Sterling Morrison, Maureen Tucker)
Recorded May 29, 1968
   Hey Mr. Rain (Version I) (Reed, John Cale, Morrison, Tucker)
Recorded September 5, 1969
   Ride Into the Sun (Reed, Yule, Morrison, Tucker)
Recorded May 6, 1969
   Coney Island Steeplechase

SIDE TWO
Recorded December 5, 1967
   Guess I'm Falling In Love (Instrumental version) (Reed, Cale, Morrison, Tucker)
Recorded May 29, 1968
   Hey Mr. Rain (Version II) (Reed, Cale, Morrison, Tucker)
Recorded June 19, 1969
   Ferryboat Bill
   Rock and Roll

seam of female singers out there who really love Nico for what she wrote and sang," he told *The Independent.* "And it's really untapped."

While it wasn't long since Reed had said that a Velvets reunion would "never happen," a lawyer hired by Cale had made good progress in unraveling the residual web of their legal and financial messes, and Reed had agreed to some compromises regarding royalties which benefited the other members. There was still simmering resentment, and many toxic words had been flung out in individual interviews over the years. Andy's death, however, changed the mood music. With precise symbolism, Reed and Cale were nudged in each other's direction by Billy Name at Warhol's memorial service. With Cale now sober and Reed perhaps less irritable than at other times, they tentatively rekindled their friendship.

The next year, Cale contacted Reed, asking him his thoughts on some pieces he was writing about Warhol, after Julian Schnabel had suggested the idea. Reed and Cale agreed they wanted to correct recent misperceptions of Andy as, in Reed's words, "a piece of fluff." They realized they could bond over their passion for this subject, this project, which became a song cycle.

Back in the Factory years, Warhol had been given the nickname Drella, by Ondine. A mash-up of Dracula and Cinderella, it was never liked by Warhol. The new songs, with writing and vocals shared, addressed Andy's relationships, work ethic, style, and worldview, sometimes from his point of view, sometimes from Lou and John's, sometimes from the perspective of others. Generally moving in chronological order of events, the *Songs for Drella* album was widely acclaimed, with *Spin* calling it "a moving testament to one of the Sixties' most important icons." Cale thought it was "reporting how misfits get together and create art," a phrase which might also serve as a nutshell reference to the Velvets.

Somehow, they'd collaborated on a full album for the first time since *White Light/White Heat*, but not without problems. Cale bristled at what he saw as Reed's control-freak tendencies. They did put on *Songs for Drella* together in December '89 for a four-night premiere at the Brooklyn Academy of Music, Moe Tucker joining them one night for an encore of "Pale Blue Eyes." Yet the old feuds resurfaced: Reed started claiming he'd done most of the work on the album, while Cale dryly said, "Working with Lou is never dull, but I wouldn't want to go through it again." He then promptly distracted himself by falling out with Brian Eno. In June 1990, though, all four surviving original Velvets—Lou, John, Sterling, and Maureen—attended the opening of the Cartier Foundation's Andy Warhol Foundation, outside Paris. Something convivial must have been in the air, because after Reed and Cale played some *Drella* songs, all four, to startled onlookers, performed an improvised, unrehearsed, fifteen-minute version of "Heroin." "That was extraordinary," said a clearly moved Reed. "I'm overcome with emotion," added Cale. Morrison said, "Not bad. Was I in tune?"

The four hung out more, even visiting the Louvre as a group, before solo business like Reed's *Magic and Loss* album took priority again. That 1992 work mused over mortality, and the same year he and Sylvia Morales divorced after twelve years' marriage. What with these and other more pragmatic, financial developments, the unlikely reunion was now likely. By mid '93, they'd found a reason, and to the unbridled glee of multiple generations of fans and a now gushingly onside media, toured again.

Lou had joked that they should play Madison Square Garden for a million dollars. This only fed the momentum. He and Sterling guested at a New York gig of John's, and in November '92 John revealed on *The Tonight Show* that the Velvets were rehearsing and the resurrection was on.

"It was pride that kept us apart," Sterling told *Rolling Stone*'s David Fricke. "But it was also pride that made us do well. Nobody cares more about our legacy than we do." He admitted the only Lou album he'd owned was *Transformer*. He still didn't quit his tugboat job; he simply took a couple of months off. Like Moe, he really needed the money. And on June 1, 1993, in Edinburgh, the European tour took off, playing, with Luna as support act, to sold-out crowds in major cities in the UK, Holland, Germany, Switzerland, Czech Republic, and France (with the Paris shows filmed). Cale sang most of the previously Nico-voiced songs. They then joined U2's *Zoo TV* tour for five dates in Italy, with many journalists questioning the wisdom of their doffing the cap to U2, before managing a messy set at the Glastonbury Festival. They were cover stars again. The album from the Paris shows even offered a brand new song, "Coyote." Cale was keen that they should create more new material; his hope wasn't matched by the others. American dates were planned, but they never got there. Surprise—everyone fell out again. Reed had seemed aloof throughout the touring experience, giving off the impression that he almost considered the others his backing band. Sterling (whose musicianship was acclaimed by reviewers) felt aggrieved at Reed's guitar roadies treating him as if of minor significance. Even Cale, who thought he'd deduced how to Reed-whisper in recent years, was enraged when Reed insisted he himself produced any mooted new recordings. Ultimately, in a very nineties sequence which you wouldn't have seen back in 1960s Manhattan, the band broke up via a series of irate faxes.

So the climax was bathos, but at least now the legend, the fantasy of The Velvet Underground could be allowed to keep growing without its actual builders tripping over themselves to get in the way. The reunion hadn't been a debacle, far from it—despite some dubious choices of leather blousons—but it had wobbled the mystique, muddied the mythology. As Lou said in 1993, though, "The proof is in the work, and the work is on record."

Sterling hadn't been in perfect health during the reunion tour, and having returned to Poughkeepsie he was diagnosed with non-Hodgkin lymphoma in late '94. He died, a day after his fifty-third birthday, on August 30, 1995. Lou Reed wrote a truly moving eulogy in *The New York Times*: "Sterling said the cancer was like leaves in the fall, a perfect Morrison description: he loved the English language." He described Sterling's pain and courage, which he'd witnessed upon last taking a train to visit him. "His eyes were as alert and clear as any eyes I've seen in this world. Not once did he complain. We spoke of music and old band mates. We talked baseball. We never spoke of what was going on." He went on to praise "funny, brilliant" Sterling's "warrior heart." Upon leaving, Lou reflected that they'd never play guitar together again. "No more Nico. No more Andy. No more Sterl." The next time he played "Sweet Jane" live, he hoped Sterling would hear the chords. "After all, he was the first one who heard the song the night I wrote it, more than 25 years ago, in the summer, before the leaves fell in the fall."

Upon the Velvets' 1996 induction (by Patti Smith) into the Rock and Roll Hall of Fame, Reed, Cale, and Tucker played the new song "Last Night I Said Goodbye to My Friend," dedicating it to Sterling.

He was survived by Martha, who he'd married in 1971, and his son and daughter. And his music.

That was it for the Velvets. On the forty-fifth anniversary of their forming, Reed, Tucker, and Doug Yule gave an interview together at the New York Public Library. Anniversary box sets and out-takes or live tracks continue to surface in various forms or permutations: *The Complete Matrix Tapes*, released in 2015, from 1969 San Francisco shows, is a must-have.

In 2009, Cale, who'd once told *The South Bank Show* that "any band telling a record company they were influenced by the Velvet Underground would be stupid," represented Wales at the Venice Biennale with *Dark Days*, a multimedia presentation looking at his relationship with his motherland. The following year, he was awarded an OBE. The *Extra Playful* EP in 2011 saw him executing art rock in an energized, fun, smart, and sexy manner. "Say hello to the future," he sang, "say goodbye to the past." His most recent solo album, *M:FANS*, released in 2016, saw him softening toward Lou ("from sadness came the strength of fire," he stated).

In 2017, he helped mark the fiftieth anniversary of the Velvets' debut with a performance of the album at Liverpool's Sound City festival, before what critic Dave Simpson referred to as "an air-punching, banana-pelting crowd of 11,000." Reviewers in general weren't dazzled by the sound quality and the randomness of guests like The Kills' Alison Mosshart, Wild Beasts, Fat White Family, and Nadine Shah, but it did emphasize the ongoing allure of the Velvets to younger generations, and a thirty-minute finale of "Sister Ray" prompted *The Guardian* to write, "Perhaps some aspects of The Velvet Underground remain too dangerous for mass consumption after all."

In 2014, *Rolling Stone* reported that Doug Yule was working "as a luthier, building and repairing violins, violas and other orchestral stringed instruments, in Seattle." Moe Tucker, they added, was residing, retired, in Douglas, Georgia, "where she has peppered her home with reminders of the Velvet Underground. 'I have pictures of the band around the house, not posed pictures . . . I don't sit and brood, but I do think about the band.'" Her support of the Tea Party and outspoken antipathy toward Barack Obama lost her some sympathy from fans.

Reed, becoming a fan of tai chi and selling designer eyewear, kept touring and releasing variable, never dull, sometimes vital albums (discussed earlier), until his death, aged seventy-one, on October 27, 2013. He'd suffered from hepatitis and diabetes for years, and his passing came five months after a liver transplant to treat liver cancer. His widow, artist and musician Laurie Anderson, who'd married him in 2008, hailed him as "a prince and a fighter." When the Grammy Awards gave the Velvets a salute, John Cale, with Moe Tucker in his lineup, performed "Sunday Morning" and "I'm Waiting for the Man." "The world has lost a fine songwriter and poet," he posted on Facebook when he heard of Reed's death. "I've lost my schoolyard buddy." A year later *The Guardian* reported that Reed's estate totaled $30 million, over half of which went to Anderson, though plenty was left too to his sister, Margaret, "to care for their mother." "The fortune speaks of careful management, for he never had a break-out US hit. His biggest album in the US, *Sally Can't Dance*, reached no higher than No. 10, and he stalled his commercial momentum by following it with *Metal Machine Music*, four sides of white noise."

Andy Warhol remains possibly the most celebrated artist of modern times, constantly applauded for his prescience as we immerse ourselves deeper in our screens and narcissism. While The Velvet Underground's profile in popular culture in the twenty-first century may not match that of The Beatles, the Stones, Dylan, Velvets fan Bowie, and (you can argue over the) others, their legacy, too, is both sprawling and monumental. The Todd Haynes documentary, rich with interviews and never-before-seen footage, fanned the flames, as did the Tate London's vast Warhol exhibition and its Factory films.

They still flow outside the mainstream, their impact on art rock, indie, goth, and any music which might be shoved under the "alternative" umbrella still resonating, with countless crusaders of cool profoundly indebted to their pioneering perversity. They rerouted the very consciousness of music with subversion of sound and a reformation of words. They hit it sideways. And through all tomorrow's parties, they're sticking with you.

In 2004, I asked Lou Reed if it was true he'd once claimed he was "too smart and literate to be the godfather of punk." "I said that??" His voice rose. "No, no way—come on, you can't believe that shit, you know that ain't true. Why would I say that? That's crazy. Look at what I write." He was keener to enthuse about the technicalities of sound quality, his loathing of George W. Bush, and OutKast's hit single "Hey Ya!"—"it's so smart, God, it's perfect pop. You hear that and you feel good."

Did he still abide by Warhol's work ethic?

"I'm not even close," he sighed. "Much as I try, much as I'm busy, I could never match that."

And after a discussion of his literary heroes (Selby, Chandler, Delmore Schwartz), he professed that he took their range onboard, "then naturally you try and go your own way. Or at least I hope I did. I saw these giants, and . . ."

Aimed high?

"Mmm. And low. High and low both."

In his book *Popism*, Warhol recalls hearing, in late 1967, a "young kid" being asked which rock group should be booked for a prestigious happening. The kid says, "There is only one rock group—the Velvet Underground."

SOURCES & PICTURE CREDITS

Books

Andy Warhol, *The Philosophy Of Andy Warhol*, PENGUIN

Andy Warhol & Pat Hackett, *Popism*, PENGUIN

Victor Bockris & Gerard Malanga, *Up-Tight: The Story of The Velvet Underground*, OMNIBUS

Peter Doggett, *Lou Reed: The Defining Years*, OMNIBUS

Anthony De Curtis, *Lou Reed: A Life*, LITTLE BROWN

Victor Bockris, *Transformer: The Complete Lou Reed Story*, HARPER COLLINS

Albin Zak (Editor), *The Velvet Underground Companion: Four Decades of Commentary* , OMNIBUS

Peter Hogan, *The Rough Guide To The Velvet Underground*, ROUGH GUIDES

Lou Reed, *I'll Be Your Mirror: The Collected Lyrics*, FABER & FABER

Chris Roberts, *A Walk on the Wilde Side: The Stories Behind the Songs*, LIMELIGHT

Jean Stein (& George Plimpton), *Edie: An American Biography*, PIMLICO

Michael Wrenn, *Lou Reed: Between The Lines*, PLEXUS

Magazines & newspapers

Melody Maker, NME, Rolling Stone, Disc & Music Echo, Spin, Uncut, Mojo, Record Collector, Sounds, The Times, The Guardian, Village Voice

Picture insert

1t, 1b, 2t: Adam Ritchie/Redferns/Getty; 2b: Tim Boxer/Hulton Archive/Getty; 3t: Michael Ochs Archives/Getty; 3b: Jack Mitchell/Getty; 4: Michael Ochs Archives/Getty; 6t: Gijsbert Hanekroot/Redferns/Getty; 6b: Bettmann/Getty; 7t: Jean-Claude Francolon/Gamma-Rapho/Getty; 7b: Rob Verhorst/Redferns/Getty; 8t: Mitchell Gerber/Corbis/VCG/Getty; 8b: Peter Pakvis/Redferns/Getty

5: Herve Gloaguen/Gamma-Rapho/Getty; 6: Bridgeman Images; 14: Bettmann/Getty; 22: TCD/Prod.DB/Alamy; 46: John Springer Collection/Corbis/Getty; 70: Blank Archives/Getty; 94: Album/Alamy; 112: Albertson, Jeff. The Velvet Underground. Jeff Albertson Photograph Collection (PH 57). Special Collections and University Archives, University of Massachusetts Amherst Libraries; 126: GAB Archive/Redferns/Getty; 142: Michael Ochs Archives/Getty; 174: Herbie Knott/Shutterstock